Teaching Humanities
in the Microelectronic Age

Teaching Humanities in the Microelectronic Age

Anthony Adams
and
Esmor Jones

THE OPEN UNIVERSITY PRESS
Milton Keynes

The Open University Press
A division of
Open University Educational Enterprises Limited
12 Cofferidge Close
Stony Stratford
Milton Keynes MK11 1BY, England

First published 1983

British Library Cataloguing in Publication Data

Adams, Anthony
Teaching humanities in the microelectronic age.
1. Humanities—Data processing
I. Title   II. Jones, Esmor
001.3'028'54   AZ105

ISBN 0-335-10196-8

The cover design shows (on the right) a section of Virgil's Aeneid: a text which
encompasses the teaching of history and religion, literature and classics. (Reproduced by
courtesy of Oxford University Press.) On the left is a section of the circuitry of a micro
computer, a tool used increasingly for teaching the very subjects listed above.

Text design by W.A.P.
Phototypeset by Getset (BTS) Ltd, Eynsham, Oxford.
Printed in Great Britain by St Edmundsbury Press, Bury St Edmunds, Suffolk.

Contents

Preface

One small reflection on the pace of change is that the authors of this book did not appreciate each other's developing interest in the possibilities of microelectronics until some time in 1980. We had both, of course, been aware, in a vague sort of way, that there were such things as computers; they were, we supposed, 'number crunchers' for boffins. Indeed, one of us actually opposed the purchase of such an educationally irrelevant machine for his University Department of Education.

This blindness could not persist as we came across so much evidence of microprocessors in everyday life — the Space Invader games, the appearance of the cheap personal micro, computerized tills in shops, and cash dispensers on bank walls. We also became aware of the beginnings of school interest in computers and the growing numbers taking Computer Studies courses. Then came the BBC series *The Mighty Micro* (and Christopher Evan's book). We became sure that we had to be involved.

The first important practical consequence of our new-found concern was the bringing together in Cambridge of a number of educationists, teachers and publishers for a weekend in October 1981. The Seminar was sponsored by Bryanston Audiovision Ltd, a small company specializing in the production of educational AV material and concerned about the future of this simple technology. The Seminar brief was to look at the possibilities opening up in the Humanities and also the dangers, to see if it might be possible to outline a coherent approach to technological change in accord with a philosophy of education rooted in the Humanities, and to suggest the kinds of material that would help schools to make educationally effective use of microelectronics. We reprint as Appendix 1 the report of that Seminar (written by Patrick Scott).

So far, there have been two direct consequences of the Seminar. One is this book. The other is FACTFILE (discussed fully in Chapter V) which resulted from the participation of Cambridge University Press and Bob Coates of MEP. There is still a great deal of work to be done — particularly in the production of good programs for classroom use. It is our hope that this book will not only stimulate some very necessary discussion among teachers of the Humanities but will also lead to useful work in producing relevant classroom materials.

We are extremely anxious that microelectronics should not become the preserve of the few for all our lives are already being affected and will continue to be affected as the pace of change increases. We cannot afford a generation of children growing up without understanding and thus without the ability properly to control their own destinies. It is in the belief that schools must have a major role in ensuring that microelectronics are developed for the benefit of us all, that we have written this book.

Anthony Adams
Esmor Jones

Acknowledgements

No book of this kind could be written without a great deal of help from people actively engaged in both computers and in education. With much pleasure, then, we would like publicly to say thank you to a number of people who, whether they knew it or not, have contributed.

First of all, we are grateful to the various schools who welcomed us and showed us what they were doing and thinking. In particular, we are grateful to Ron Jones, who, as we later explain, gave us our first experience of children enjoying working with a computer and subsequently pointed us very much in the most fruitful educational directions. We are grateful too to Daniel Chandler for many hours of discussion, for his patience with our own first fumbling attempts at hands-on experience and, especially, for his major contribution to our own thinking about the impact of microelectronics on education. We are similarly grateful to Patrick Scott, who also wrote the report on the Bryanston Seminar published in this volume as an Appendix. As the impetus for this book (and much else) came from that Seminar, we must also express our gratitude to all the participants in that seminal weekend.

We would also like to express our gratitude to Ken Bingham at the Cambridge University Department of Education who helped us and supported us technically as we looked at both hardware and software in the Department's Computer room. We are also grateful to Linda Allen for the accuracy of her typing of our chapters — work done under considerable pressure of time.

Finally, we must thank John Skelton of the Open University Press (himself a participant in the Bryanston Seminar) and his colleagues for both thinking the central issues of this book to be important and then insuring so rapid and efficient journey to publication.

1

The Microcomputer and the Classroom

> It was after watching BBC television's Horizon programme, 'Now the Chips are Down', that my staff and I — a team of primary school teachers which prided itself on teaching children the process skills needed to cope with a rapidly changing society — realized that here in this programme was a window on tomorrow's world: a world which none of us could recognize. In our rural school on the very edge of the Fens the chip had passed us by!

With these words, Ron Jones, then Head Teacher of Upwood County Primary School in Cambridgeshire, opened his now seminal study, *Microcomputers: Their Uses in Primary Schools.*[1] Since then he has been responsible for much of the thinking and innovation that has gone into the development of primary school applications for microcomputers over the last two years. He founded in 1981, and chairs, the influential organization, Micros and Primary Education (MAPE).

In 1978, when he and his staff saw the Horizon programme to which he refers, as he would be the first to admit, they knew very little about this new technology, which, as a result of their later discussions, was to move towards the very core of their curriculum. About this time, too, we, flushed with the enthusiasm generated by our recent purchase of a Sinclair ZX80 computer, were beginning, however hesitantly, to ask ourselves questions about what we could do in the classroom with what was for us still a new, almost magical, and certainly mysterious, piece of equipment. We began to make enquiries about where we could go to see microcomputers in action in the classroom. Not surprisingly, the trail led us to Upwood County Primary School where we received a warm welcome from Ron Jones and first saw children at work with a microcomputer. The first classroom we went into was an infant room where five-year-olds were learning keyboard skills from a very simple program which generated a random series of letters on the screen and asked the pupils to respond by typing the same letter on the Commodore Pet keyboard — a gift to the school from a parent who had replaced it by a more powerful machine. The motivation for the children was provided by an entertaining piece of

1

graphics which showed a cat chasing a mouse. The faster and more accurately the pupils typed away, the further the mouse got away from the cat. If they gave an inaccurate or slow response the cat caught up until, as it caught the mouse, the word MUNCH appeared in large letters on the screen. Since this was the first time that either of us had seen a microcomputer bigger than our Sinclair we found the demonstration absorbing, entertaining, and thought-provoking. One of the things we learned as we watched was that the five-year-olds, when they became bored by the task, varied it by deliberately giving the wrong response so that the cat would catch the mouse and enjoy its meal! Already one of the lessons they were learning was how to outwit the programmer's intentions, to make the micro do what they wanted rather than the other way around. Most impressive of all was the ease and confidence with which they approached the machine, a startling contrast with their regular class teacher and with our own fumbling steps towards gaining what we later came to call 'hands on' experience. They were also learning the letters of the alphabet, of course, but they were learning them in the way in which they are arranged on a typewriter keyboard and acquiring the psycho-motor skills of handling a keyboard and reading a screen (to which they were expected to make a response) in the process. Such children, starting school in 1980, were already being prepared for the world they will go into as school leavers in the 1990s. The one thing that is quite certain about that world is that it will be very different from that which any of those teaching them at present can possibly envisage.

After that initial visit to Ron Jones's school we went to see many others, where, it was reported to us, interesting work was taking place. Not unexpectedly, what we saw ranged from the first-class to the dreadful, and invariably it was the quality of the *educational* thinking behind the use of the microcomputer that made the difference. To use the equipment constructively in the classroom, teachers and pupils had to ask some significant questions about what the whole operation was seeking to achieve. A group of children in a school in the West Midlands, for example (yet another junior school with an innovative headteacher), was working on the returns from the 1851 census, which are now available as a computerized data-bank. They, too, were using a Commodore Pet, though this time with disc drive so that they could access the census returns very speedily, and the data-processing facilities that it provided enabled them to call up, for example, all the nail-makers in a particular road at the time of the census, or to discover the occupations in a particular area of all males between the ages of 25 and 41, or any other particular combinations of information of this kind. They also had available to them a range of historical resource materials, ranging from history textbooks suited to their reading level to a map of their area showing land uses at the time the census was taking place. Their teacher's comment was that this was a way of making history vividly alive for eight-year-olds; now it became a story about real people who had lived a hundred years ago in streets they walked along every day. They could discover in considerable detail who had lived in a particular house, how crowded it had been, what the ages of the inhabitants were, what jobs they did. Of course, all this information could have been discovered from the pages of the census returns themselves, seen in facsimile photostat, but only at the expense of many hours of labour and the effort of reading minuscule and difficult handwriting. Having the information stored on disc with a program that made it possible to combine and compare various facets of the information made the task much more possible for junior school children. It took the drudgery out of this kind of historical investigation. (Though, it should be added, the facsimile photostats of the actual census returns were there in the classroom as well; the children were never allowed to forget the actual primary source from which the data-base had been compiled.) One thing that they decided they wanted to know about was the school population in their own home area of Brierley Hill at the time. As soon as they began to explore this, interesting and surprising facts came to light. There seemed, for example, a surprising number of 14-year-olds described as 'scholars', that is still in school attendance, in 1851. It wasn't until they came to check these figures from the census returns as shown on their viewing screen against other documents they had amongst their resources, such as school attendance registers and mining payrolls, that the real truth began to emerge. Recent legislation, in the form of the Mines Act, had made it illegal to send fourteen-year-olds down the pits. Many, reported to the enumerators as 'scholars', appeared in no school lists but did appear in the payrolls. A little thought enabled the pupils to derive a possible (and likely) answer to the paradox. Clearly the head of the household had been lying in his returns to the enumerator to avoid getting himself into trouble and risking his son or daughter losing a job!

What were these students now — the eight-year-olds in 1982 — learning? As already suggested, they were learning that history was about real people, whole families that they could identify and whose stories they could follow through, using the various data and resources of a primary and secondary nature available to them. But they were also learning that, in order to make effective use of such resources, whether on the computer file or in print, they must first learn how to formulate the right questions to discover what it was they wanted to know. Indeed, defining as precisely as possible what it was that they wanted to know was a necessary preliminary to asking the right questions. Important study skills, necessary if our pupils are to develop as autonomous learners through whatever medium they employ, and which on the whole we are notoriously bad at teaching, were beginning to be learned by the eight-year-olds working at their computer terminal. Also, however, they were learning to use and *to take for granted* the way in which such information is actually stored and made accessible for research purposes in the world outside school. They were, in effect, learning the research methodology of the twentieth century.

But they were also learning other things, equally important to anyone who is beginning to understand the nature of historical research and thinking. They were discovering how important it was not to believe what they saw in a single piece of evidence, whether it was a handwritten census return, or something that appeared on a screen, or as part of a computer print-out. They were learning about such things as provenance, how to judge the authenticity of a piece of evidence, how to weigh one piece of evidence against another, how to make intelligent guesses and derive ways of testing them, how (ultimately) to make their own historical judgements. And, in conducting this kind of historical investigation, they were using exactly the same materials and methods of study as are available to a professional historical researcher. Instead of learning their history at second-hand these children were able to go directly to primary source materials to see how they could be used and how to recognize when the apparent answers they received to their questions needed fuller and more complex investigation to make sense as the total picture of the jigsaw they were piecing together was revealed. In other words, at eight, these children were learning what it is to think like a historian. And all this was only possible because most of the data they needed had been put onto a computer disc so that the donkey work of the research was already done for them. They were set free from the processing of mere information in order to think. This liberation of the student from the routine drudgery of much of traditional learning processes seems to us one of the most important functions of the microcomputer in the classroom. Used properly, it can create 'space' in which young minds can be taught to think and explore ideas for themselves.

Our next example is taken from the opposite end of the educational system, from a sixth form college in fact. Here a talented young English teacher was concerned to develop skills of comprehension within a genuinely case-study based approach. What he did was to take the housing regulations of a Local Authority and to create files on three imaginary families, all of whom were applicants for authority-subsidized housing. The students' first task was to work out the order in which these families would appear in the priority list for the subsidized housing that was available in terms of the Authority's regulations. This meant interpretating the regulations (itself a highly complex reading task) and extracting from the case studies the relevant information to provide the data to work out where each family stood in terms of their priority rating.

Many skills were needed here: careful interpretation of complex and varied written materials and quite sophisticated mathematical calculations. The last of these, in terms of the mechanical process involved, was taken care of by the computer program that the teacher had devised to assist the pupils. This meant that they were free to concentrate upon the real conceptual tasks involved: to extract the relevant information they needed from the case histories, to input the data they had derived from these into the computer, to read from the computer print-out the results derived from the data they had entered, to draw appropriate conclusions from this set of results, and, finally, to write letters to the heads of the households concerned to explain to them in clear English why they were, or were not, eligible for subsidized housing. As in the junior school, the donkey work, the purely mechanical part of the exercise, could be done for them more quickly and accurately than they could have done it themselves, by the computer. They were free to think their way through the problem presented to them and to simulate something amounting to what might be a real-life office situation of this kind. (The simulation became even more realistic when the letters were written by the class as a whole drafting them on the computer, used in the mode of word processor. Interestingly, too, as part of the exercise they had to turn the information they had derived from the computer into plain English that would be understood in text form by a member of the general public.) This development of higher-order reading and writing skills seems to us part, at least, of what our English programmes in schools should be about.

A not dissimilar exercise was carried out by a student of ours working with a third-year remedial group in an urban comprehensive school. The school's English syllabus required them to learn to write letters of applications for jobs (not particularly motivating for the fourteen-year-old in an area where jobs are increasingly hard to come by). They had available a number of free pamphlets from the Youth Employment Service describing possible jobs and listing the kinds of interests and qualifications that were desirable in applicants for them. Using a not very complicated data-base sorting program, the student-teacher was able to produce a package which enabled the students to input their own interest and (hoped for) qualifications and to obtain from the screen information about the possible range of jobs that might interest them. They were then set to compose a curriculum vitae and an appropriate letter of application being 'prompted' by the computer program with requests for their NAME, D o B, ADDRESS and so on, until, in the end, they had a beautifully printed-out version of the work they had been engaged on. What had previously been a mere drudgery to them became something that was 'fun', something, in fact, to which they returned during non-lesson time to continue working at, and something that gave them a sense of satisfaction in seeing the work they had composed emerging finally in a correct and well-presented format. (The sense of achievement among these remedial pupils was summed up by one of them when he said: 'My brother's 16 and even he hasn't used a computer yet!'.) In the process, also, they had been doing a good deal of 'reading' (skimming, scanning, browsing) amongst the careers publications that they had spurned as 'boring' in the first instance.

Several lessons seem to us to emerge from this example. First of all there is the importance of not restricting the use of the computer to the 'more able', more academically-inclined pupils. Many years ago we were arguing the case for the use of the typewriter in the remedial class; the same seems even more true about the use of the microcomputer today. Alongside providing a sense of achievement there is also a strong sense of motivation that results from its use — the pull of the video game illustrates this only too clearly. But, like the primary school pupils in our first example, these students were learning modern office skills of using a keyboard and reading a screen that might, conceivably, be of some use to them if they eventually found a job to go to.

As in so many of the other examples we have given in this chapter the use of the computer to get rid of the drudgery, in this case of the process of drafting and redrafting, is important. Both Seymour Papert and Frank Smith have recently paid tribute to the function of the computer-as-word-processor in the classroom:

> For most children rewriting a text is so laborious that the first draft is the final copy, and the skill of reading with a critical eye is never acquired . . .
> This changes dramatically when children have access to computers capable of manipulating text . . . I have seen a child move from total rejection of writing to an intense involvement (accompanied by rapid improvement of quality) within a few weeks of beginning to write with a computer. (S. Papert)[2]

We shall have more to say about this important function of the microprocessor in a later chapter. For these remedially diagnosed pupils, in particular, they were released, possibly for the first time, from the drudgery and sheer physical difficulty of writing, so that they could concentrate upon what was being written and how it was being composed, and still emerge with a satisfying and finished product at the end.

Our final example of the liberating effect the microcomputer can have in the classroom is taken from the middle years of schooling. It illustrates how children can be helped to learn classification skills that would not easily fit into any kind of conventionally timetabled subject in the curriculum even though they are skills necessary for analytical exploration in virtually every subject we teach. It is one of a family of games for the computer derived from the old party game, *Animal, Vegetable and Mineral*. This version, entitled *Creatures*, was especially devised for schools by Daniel Chandler and is best described in his own words:

> The computer asks for the players to think of a living creature and then tries to guess what it might be. It asks, 'Is it an insect?', 'Is it a fish?' and so on, imitating the human technique of narrowing the options. The computer has very little chance, in fact, at the beginning of the game since . . . it knows only thirteen creatures. What is interesting about the game is that when the computer admits defeat the students have to tell it what the creature is, and frame a question that would distinguish their choice from the computer's last guess. In this game the students are 'teaching' the computer because it stores

and uses the new questions. In the process students have to devise questions
involving increasingly subtle distinctions.

To illustrate how the game proceeds and to show just how challenging it
can be, here is how some student teachers . . . quickly found themselves in
rather a tight spot:

CREATURES

THINK OF A LIVING CREATURE
AND THE COMPUTER WILL TRY TO
GUESS WHAT IT IS.

IF IT DOES NOT GUESS IT, YOU
WILL HAVE TO TEACH THE
COMPUTER.
ARE YOU THINKING OF A CREATURE?
YES

IS IT AN INSECT? NO
IS IT A FISH? NO
IS IT A BIRD? YES
IS IT A BIRD OF PREY? YES
IS IT A KESTREL? NO

THE CREATURE YOU WERE THINKING
OF WAS A ? HAWK

PLEASE TYPE A QUESTION THAT
WOULD DISTINGUISH A HAWK FROM
A KESTREL . . .

. . . Here is an excellent program to generate constructive discussion, re-
quiring students to make effective use of reference sources and to take great
care in the framing of questions. It also acts as a dynamic demonstration of
the way in which language fashions information into 'trees' of inter-related
classifications . . . This game would provide an ideal opportunity . . . [to
help students] . . . develop what is surely the most important learning skill
of all: the ability to ask the most significant questions. (D. Chandler)[3]

In the visit to Ron Jones's school that we spoke of earlier, we saw a group
of nine-year-olds playing a simpler version of this game and saw them sur-
rounded by reference books which they were consulting avidly in their attempts to solve the difficult problems of classification that had been left for
them by a previous group that had been playing the game.

All of the illustrations given above of the use of microcomputers in
humanities classrooms are far removed from the kind of thing that is currently
available in many commercially produced 'software' programs.

All too often in such cases, instead of the microcomputer being seen as a facilitator of the learning process, a way of creating the conditions in which learning can effectively take place, often using group interaction as a significant part of the learning process, the computer becomes itself a mediator of instructional programs, a more up-to-date and complex version of the teaching machine or the language laboratory. Typical of the kind of programs in computer-assisted-learning (CAL) that are being developed at the moment, especially in North America (though see also the Sinclair *Fun to Learn* series as a good example of inadequate home-produced 'educational' software), is the adaptation of badly thought-through workbook exercises (what Americans call 'busywork') to become equally bad computer programs.

> How strange it is that computers in education should so often reduce to using bright new gadgets to teach the same old stuff in thinly disguised versions of the same old way. (Papert and Solomon)[4]

At a recent conference on reading that one of us attended in Portland, Oregon, the publishers' exhibition was filled with countless examples of this kind of program, complete with young children working away at every terminal with all the absorption of people playing Pacman or Space Invaders. One such program, for example, generated a series of words on the screen together with five possible multiple choice alternatives. The task of the respondent was to pick the opposite of the word shown. One of the frames presented the word WHITE with, as possible opposites, the words: YELLOW, GREEN, PURPLE, BLACK and RED. Presumably the word being sought was BLACK. This seems an almost perfect example of the computer being used to no discernible purpose at all, with the ill thought-through answer an example not only of bad English teaching but bad Physics teaching also. The really worrying thing about programs of this kind is that they can (especially when supported by visually exciting graphics) be just as motivating and compulsive to those working on them as the more imaginative and educationally sounder programs we have been describing earlier. This is why it becomes essential to think through on clear educational grounds what we are seeking to achieve rather than to just accept the computer into the classroom as the latest of the 'bright new gadgets' that will do the work of instruction for us. Fubini makes the same point as Papert when he states: 'I am opposed to using the new technologies mainly as direct substitutes for old methods.' The real development comes educationally 'when we employ the discovery to do something *new in a new way*'.[5] This seems to us what we should be on the verge of doing in seeking to explore the educational importance of microcomputers to humanities teaching at present.

This chapter has sought to set the scene. It makes clear why we feel that the time has now arrived when a book such as this needs to be written. The new technology is with us and will not go away. We must be alert to its possibilities and its very real dangers so far as education is concerned. The rest of the book seeks to help teachers formulate their own criteria so as to be able to judge on educational grounds the directions in which we are being led, and to help teachers themselves to play a part in determining the direction in which they wish to travel. In the end, any book on computers and education will need to be more about education than about the 'gadgetry' of the computers.

2

Computers all Around Us

The context in which the educational thinking needs to take place is that of enormous and far-reaching changes in society, the consequence of what is becoming conventionally known as 'the third wave'. By this is meant the notion that we have passed through three technological revolutions. The first, the Industrial Revolution, was one in which machines extended the muscular power of man; the second, the Electronic Revolution, saw an extension of our nervous systems with the development of radio, film and television; now, with the third, the Information Revolution, machines, in the shape of computers, are extending our brain power. Because we are experiencing it as we write and are, consequently, so firmly embedded in it, it is sometimes difficult for us to realize the speed at which this latest revolution is taking place. It does, however, come as something of a shock to realize that it was not until 1970 that the pocket calculator was invented and that the microcomputer itself is not yet ten years old. A good example of the speed at which such development is taking place is provided by the High Street shops, the local travel agent for example. One such shop, known to us, did not even have a simple electronic calculator on the premises about six years ago; now, in the same shop, every sales assistant's desk has its own small computer terminal and the shop has immediate telex communication with hotels and airlines all over the world. It still comes as something of a shock to realize that, should there be any doubt about a client's credit worthiness, the state, for instance, of his American Express account can be instantly checked by a telephone call to Brighton and thereafter by satellite communication between Brighton, England and Phoenix, Arizona — all done so quickly and efficiently that the customer is probably not even aware that it is taking place. Still more of a surprise is to go to another travel agent, say in Toronto, and discover that the computer in the office there can track down instantly through the airline computer the whole of one's travelling history, even down to the name and telex number of the High Street travel agent with whom the whole process began. Ten years ago this would have seemed like magic; now we take it for granted as part of the normal way in which our everyday lives are organized. More important for us to recognize, as educators, is that young people leaving school and getting jobs in offices such as this travel agent's are going into their working lives when the potentiality of this kind of technology, and the flow of information which it makes possible, is taken for granted. From the beginning of their working lives they are hearing all around them what is to many of us a strange new language ('Electronic Newspeak' as someone has entertainingly dubbed it) — a language of bits and bytes, chips and floppies, VDUs and interfaces. This is now the language that any young person leaving school is likely to have to pick up in the first few days of being in any job, especially in the information providing and using or the service industries. We have deliberately tried to write this book in non-technical language but it is becoming increasingly difficult to survive in today's world without acquiring at least a smattering of the language of the new technology. The universal prevalence of the Electronic Newspeak and the imperceptible ease with which we are all gliding into using its terminology itself shows how swiftly and unnoticedly the world around us is changing. Later we shall need to ask whether our educational institutions are changing so as to keep pace with these fundamental changes taking place around us. At present we are concerned merely to chronicle the change and note some of its implications for our major theme.

There has been, in this country, because of a complex interaction of political and economic forces, an attempt to resist the implications of these changes but, within the last year, further significant changes have taken place and, again, are most easily seen in the local High Street. It is within the last few years that the Post Office has begun to approve and install (albeit somewhat grudgingly) some of the newer equipment that should make our lives easier: answering machines and self-dialling telephones, for example. We now have electronic clocks that will time our calls for us and give us a print out of the charges incurred in making a call. We are just beginning, again belatedly, to take for granted radio telephones which can be used up to something like 40 miles from their home base. In Boots and W. H. Smith (in every reasonably-sized town) there are now at least two makes of home computer at prices well under £100. The Sinclair ZX81 was one of the most fashionable of Christmas presents for small children only a year ago. In the United States, according to an article in *Time* magazine, sales of home computers are expected to explode from 'a mere 35,000 in 1980 to 1.5 million in 1983'. Alongside this explosion in sales has gone an extraordinary war of price cutting of which we are only seeing the beginning in the United Kingdom. This is not, however, without its ultimate cost, as *Time* points out:

> Manufacturers have been able to chop prices drastically primarily because the computer keyboard console is only the first of a series of items that buyers need. At a minimum, they must also have television sets or special video screens to display whatever the keyboard unit is doing, and software programs for the machines. Many customers also buy printers, memory

boosters, telephone links, power cords and numerous other devices. The real
cost of a computer often comes from these additional components. Industry
experts compare buying a home computer with buying a razor. The initial
cost is small, but the total outlay is much higher because of the later spending
on blades. Notes Computer Analyst David Wu of Montgomery Securities in
San Francisco: 'They give people a cheap machine, and then they get them
with the add-ons. It's like opium'. [1]

The article goes on to stress that, although many of the owners of these home
computers use them only for playing games, others 'are branching into fields
that include language learning, music writing, investment analysis'.

Some analysts believe that the potential for home computers has hardly been
tapped. Many expect consumers to begin banking and shopping through
them soon. Others stress the value of electronic data banks that offer huge
storehouses of information.

Since that article was published there has been announced in November
1982 the beginnings in the Sutton Coldfield area of the West Midlands of a
full-blown experiment in home banking and shopping using television
Viewdata with links between homes and central mainframe computers via the
subscribers' home telephone line.

If, while we are in W. H. Smith, we care to glance at the magazine racks, the
evidence is there in plenty of the speed and significance of the growth areas of
the home video and computer market. The same shops that are selling the
home computers are selling electronic watches for a few pounds that, only two
or three years ago, would have been prohibitively expensive. Watches that, at
a touch of a button, will not only tell us the time in any part of the world but
which will also play us tunes on our birthday or wedding anniversaries, re-
mind us of appointments, and let us play Space Invaders on their obliging
dials, now themselves another form of Visual Display Unit (VDU).

Technically the flat screen TV is already with us and we are reliably informed that the next development in this field will be the folding, ultra-small
pocket VDU that we shall all be able to carry around with us. Then, potentially, at very limited cost, we shall be able to plug this into the nearest power
point (unless by this time it is being entirely solar powered) and, through any
telephone line, be able to be in instant contact with any data-bank stored
anywhere in the world. As this is written in the early part of 1983 it seems a
far off, even visionary, concept. All the signs are that it is likely to be an everyday reality shortly after this book arrives at publication.

The first thing that strikes us about all this is not just the speed at which it
is all happening (though that is remarkable enough), nor just the new language
that we have become familiar with, but the need to develop, as a matter of
urgency, new skills to make the most of the new technology that is available
to us. Whatever else Space Invaders and Pacman may or may not have done,
they have produced a whole generation of young people with remarkable

hand – eye co-ordination skills, even if of a somewhat limited immediate application. Meanwhile the term 'the new literacy' is rapidly being adopted to
describe those who have acquired the new, but now everyday, skills of using
a keyboard (quite different in many ways from conventional typing) and
reading a screen.

What we are seeing here, of course, is the outlet in the High Street, or the
shopping centre, of the consumer end of a change which is far more wide-
reaching and significant, a change that might almost be said to be affecting our
sensibilities, indeed, the whole way in which we gain our appreciation of our
world. Does the young person who possesses a digital watch, for example (and
who has probably possessed no other), have the same kind of awareness of time
as those who were brought up with conventional dials, or, now, with analogue
watches? The one seems to lead to a heightened awareness of the present
moment, the concentration upon an instant of time as the numbers flip past,
present and future as we watch the hands sweeping the dial. One might
surmise that the sense, amongst young people today, of what is meant by a
second is much sharper than when we were young, but that the passage of an
hour is a much less clear concept. It is too early to be sure how much things
are altering significantly the way in which we perceive our world but there is
some evidence that such changes in perception are taking place. Indeed,
Marshall McLuhan wrote prophetically some considerable time ago now:
'Electric information environments . . . alter our feelings and sensibilities,
especially when they are not attended to'. (our italics)[2]

It is within this context that the Department of Education and Science's
Microelectronics Education Project (MEP) has been belatedly developed. It
was announced by the Government in March 1980 and Richard Fothergill, its
Director, produced a paper outlining its basic strategy which was published in
April 1981:

> The aim of the Programme is to help schools to prepare children for life in
> a society in which devices and systems based on microelectronics are com-
> monplace and pervasive. These technologies are likely to alter the relation-
> ships between one individual and another and between individuals and their
> work; and people will need to be aware that the speed of change is acceler-
> ating and that their future careers may well include many retraining stages as
> they adjust to new technological developments.[3]

Put like this, the Programme seems to have, as we feel it should, a major concern with the areas of humanities and social studies education; in practice its
impact in those areas has so far (1983) been disappointingly small. Part of the
reason for this emerges in the account of that part of the Programme concerned with 'ways of using the computer as an aid to teaching and learning':

> In principle, software can be developed for computer-based learning across
> the curriculum, but the Programme *will give priority to applications in*

> mathematics, the sciences, craft/design technology, geography and courses related
> to business or clerical occupations. Some attention will also be given to careers
> education, languages and the humanities . . .
>
> The main focus of interest . . . will be on the secondary school curriculum
> but the Programme will be concerned to *assist appropriate developments* in
> primary and middle schools.

(Fothergill — our italics)[4]

Following this strategy the Department of Industry provided a scheme whereby at least one computer from those on an approved list would be made available to every secondary school with the Department meeting fifty per cent of the cost. Now, in the second phase of the Programme's work the proposal is the extension of the subsidy scheme to equip every primary school with a computer also.

The staff of the MEP is hardworking and dedicated to educational advance; clearly they have had to operate within the general guidelines evolved by the Departments of Education and Science and of Industry. It is our view that those guidelines are too narrow and that the whole Programme was introduced too late and on far too niggardly a scale. (However, it is encouraging to read in March 1983 of a two year extension of MEP and a doubling of its funds). Typically it started at the wrong end of the educational spectrum with the secondary school, committed for the most part to traditional subject areas within the curriculum, and not with the more open-ended and exploratory primary school. The result is easy to foresee. In the many schools that took up the Government's offer of subsidy the few computers that were introduced became the preserve of the physics and mathematics departments, and even the possibilities of a programme of 'computers across the curriculum' went virtually unexplored. Furthermore, because of the elitist structure of most mathematics and science courses, with carefully devised setting arrangements, there has been every likelihood of 'computer education', in any sense of the phrase, being restricted to the older and the more academically orientated students with very little computer education in the wider sense being practised at all. The Government strategy, like much of its strategy for education generally, has been a purely instrumental one with a concentration upon the use of computers in the workplace, an education in computers as technology in fact; there has been very little thinking given to the social education of all pupils for living in the computer age as implied by the *aims* quoted above. If they were to be taken seriously then we contend that the Programme should have had its *major* emphasis in the first instance directed towards the primary and middle years of schooling, towards the average ability student, and towards the curriculum areas of the humanities and social sciences as much as the scientifically-based areas of the curriculum. Indeed it is in recognition of the urgent need to consider the implications for the *whole* curriculum of the latest technological revolution and the conviction that the matter is too urgent and too significant to be left in the hands of a few that this book has been written. Within this whole curriculum we believe that the arts and the humanities still play a vital role and that, in this area too, the computer, properly used, can make a vitally important contribution to children's learning. Seymour Papert has suggested that the basic question for society to face in the outset of 'the third wave' is whether children in school learn to program computers and gain some understanding of how they work, or whether they are programmed for them and by those in the computer-educated élite who themselves have learned to program and to control the computer. This seems to us to have far-reaching educational implications for the kind of computer software we develop in school and we return to some of these in a later chapter.

Indeed, we may wonder, in the light of the earlier part of this chapter, whether, in the eyes of the pupils, the things currently on offer to them in schools do not have a very old-fashioned appearance; whether, in spite of the launch of the excellent BBC microcomputer, we are not still educationally in a curious Stone Age technology compared with what is already happening in the home market. There are still schools, for example, equipped with only black-and-white television (whose Governors would think the introduction of colour an unwarranted extravagance) long after colour has become the only acceptable standard in the home. Indeed, for most of the young, television without colour is not recognizable as the same thing at all. The widely-spread growth of the ownership of home video-recorders (themselves the products of the early '70s) and the increased home availability of television cameras pinpoint our virtual neglect of television education in the schools. Indeed, in many of our schools, the audio-cassette tape recorder is still seen by some teachers as the 'new technology', which makes them very odd places in which to educate the next generation of 'the third wave' in a world where the market place is so rapidly changing. However, the market-place is changing in a more significant sense also. A random culling of local newspaper advertisements for jobs as this was being written yielded the following amongst many other possibilities:

ELECTRONIC ENGINEERS

Excellent opportunities in successful local companies for electronic test-service-design engineers.

Ring now for further details. Ref 32546

SQUIRES APPOINTMENTS (AGY), A division of Anglo Appointments,
21-23 Queen Victoria Street, Reading 585522.

We need a young energetic

ELECTRONICS ENGINEER

to assist in the development of our range of medical imaging equipment. Applicants will be qualified to HNC level with practical experience in principles of electronics and microprocessor design. An ability to programme in machine language would be an advantage. Salary negotiable.

Please apply to:

Siel, Unit 8, Youngs Industrial Estate, Paices Hill, Aldermaston, Berks.

ROYAL BERKSHIRE HOSPITAL
London Road, Reading

CLERICAL OFFICER

required in the joint Public Health/Microbiology Section of the Pathology Department. Varied duties will include handling laboratory specimens and keeping numerical records. Typing and/or shorthand an advantage and experience with computers and VDUs. 37 hour week.

Salary scale £3,169 (at age 21 or over) rising to £4,394 pa.
(Pay rise pending).

UNIVERSITY OF READING
Data Processing Office

(1) FULL-TIME COMPUTER PROGRAMMER
    required for a fixed period of five years. Ref. R38A.

(2) HALF-TIME COMPUTER PROGRAMMER
    required for a fixed period of one year. Ref. R39A.

The Data Processing Office provides a computing service for the University's Administration using a Hewlett Packard 3000 Computer. Current applicants include Payroll, Accounts, Stock Control. The major project under development is an interactive Student Record system. Applicants should have at least one year's experience of COBOL programming. Knowledge of the HP3000 and interactive techniques would be an
advantage. Salary in the range of £5,500 − £8,085 pa (pro-rate for part-time).

We are all familiar by now with the many advertisements (and related jokes)
about those motor cars designed by computers and built by robots. The robot
factory is certainly no figment of the science fiction writers' imagination, a
thing of the distant future; it is precisely the environment in which those now
at school will be seeking their first jobs. Even more will be going into service
industries in which providing and using information will be of the first
importance. Chandler (1982)[5] quotes figures to show how in the United
States in 1880 about 5% of the workforce were engaged in information related
industry with about 45% engaged in agriculture; by 1980 the number of those
engaged in agriculture has shrunk to about 2% and those in information industries grown to about 47%, far more than in any other sector of the labour
economy.

This is to ignore, of course, the many others who will be leaving school with
no jobs at all to go to. The new technology has brought with it startling new
problems so far as employment is concerned. As with so much else, we are
tending to respond to the issue of employment in the same old way,
recognizing a symptom but totally mistaking the diagnosis of the problem.

It is not the case, as many young people themselves tend to think along with
their parents and teachers, that the acquisition of more qualifications will
somehow make them more eligible on the job market. It may well be, as
suggested above, that they require very different skills and thinking processes
to those they needed in the past (and which we are doing little in the schools
to equip them with) but whatever skills they acquire the jobs, in the old-
fashioned sense, will still not be there. Just as we gave several examples in the
previous chapter of the way in which the drudgery and the 'busywork' could
be taken out of learning and teaching by the application of microtechnology
so that 'space' could be created within which real thinking and learning could
go on, so, too, the same applies in industry. At present, however, we still live
in a world dominated by a work ethos and a work ethic; we tie up people's

sense of self-respect and their image of themselves with the notion of the job they do. 'What does he do for a living?' is still one of the first speculative questons we ask about someone to whom we have been introduced. For most people, also, the workplace is still the main means of social interaction outside the family. But, as other social and industrial changes are taking place without our being aware of them, so this aspect of our lives is changing also. We need urgently to recognize for schools and for society the implications of the plain fact that there will just not be enough jobs to go round in the future; it is not just a matter of economic recession that has led to the present situation. We shall have to find schemes such as job sharing to ration and share more equitably that work — in the sense of *paid* employment — that remains to do. (There is, of course, in a very different sense no real shortage of *work* in our society. There remains much to be done in such fields as the caring industries, though voluntary agencies, in the betterment of the environment and so on. What shortage there is, is of work for which people, either individually or collectively, are willing to pay, and it is unlikely that this situation will change.) Indeed, as the new technological revolution proceeds further in the next twenty years, the shortage of paid employment will become even greater. A good deal of the unskilled labour that was done in the old factories will disappear completely in the new factories, as the 'chores' of the manufacturing and distribution industries will be largely taken over by the next generation of industrial robots; the pressing of buttons on assembly lines and the taking of inventories by hand are already a thing of the past. In this sense the new technology has gone a long way towards destroying the old jobs and, in its turn, it has led to the creation of quite new jobs, such as the ones quoted in the advertisements above. But, in consequence, the gap between the skilled and the unskilled becomes even greater in this society and, interestingly enough, it is also a widening of the gap between the young and the old at the same time. The 'skilled' in this world we are now entering will be those school-leavers who have grown up with the new technology as part of their natural everyday existence. The middle-aged (their teachers) are likely to become progressively 'deskilled' as the technological revolution develops. Considerations such as this led the social anthropologist, Margaret Mead, in her important book, *Culture and Commitment* (1970), to make a useful distinction between what she called postfigurative and prefigurative cultures:

> We must . . . teach ourselves how to alter adult behavior so that we can give up postfigurative upbringing . . . and discover prefigurative ways of teaching and learning that will keep the future open. We must create new models for adults who can teach their children *not what to learn, but how to learn and not what they should be committed to but the value of commitment.*
>
> Postfigurative cultures, which focused on the elders — those who had learned the most and were able to do the most with what they had learned — were essentially closed systems that continually replicated the past. *We must now move towards the creation of open systems that focus on the future* — and so

on children, those whose capacities are least known and whose choices must
be left open. (our emphasis)[6]

What has been said and implied earlier, and will be explored in more detail
later, about 'open' styles of schooling, working in groups, helping students to
become autonomous learners, takes on a particular significance in the light of
this quotation: if we were right in our earlier suggestion that the Information
Revolution has provided us with machines, in the shape of computers, which
actually extend our brain power, then it is certainly the case that prefigurative
styles of education will become those that we shall have to rely on.

The fact that there will be less work of a traditional kind does not, of course,
mean, as some optimistic thinkers have suggested, that we shall all have more
'leisure' and that what we need to do in the schools is simply to prepare young
people for the creative use of their leisure. As Tony Watts has pointed out in
a fascinating article[7] — one of the few to have considered seriously the curriculum implications of unemployment — 'leisure' is what you have when
you have time left over from work. If you have no work to go to, this does not
mean that you have unlimited leisure; what you have is what Watts calls
'negotiable time', time which *you* must decide how to fill and use profitably.
Some of the implications of this are only just beginning to dawn on us: for
example, if there is no workplace to go to, in order to meet with other people
and to conduct social intercourse, then other institutions will have to be
provided. The nature of the traditional school may have to change to take
account of this, moving more towards the conception of the community
school, or the education and leisure centre, to provide a place for interactive
relationships with others. For this to happen as speedily as it needs to, there
will have to be important changes in the way in which 'schools' see themselves
as fulfilling their role. If the young people leaving school are going to have
more of what we have called 'negotiable time', for example, surely one of the
things that should be 'basic' in the curriculum is helping them to learn to plan
and to apportion their time accordingly. Yet the severely timetabled structure
of the traditional secondary school militates almost totally against this
possibility: we take pupils from a school environment in which every moment
of the day has been planned for them, and turn them into a world of non-work
where they find time on their hands, with no prior preparation to cope with
the skills of living that this entails. Again we have failed to appreciate the real
nature of the social and economic situation and the real nature of the problems
and the opportunities that the 'third wave' provides. Unless we can meet this
challenge, not just to the schools but to the whole of the education system in
its widest possible sense, we shall move further towards what is just beginning
to be taken for granted as the norm in our society, a society comprised of three
classes: the middle class, doing the managerial jobs and taking the decisions;
the working class, doing what of the 'chores' remain to be done; and the out-of-
work class, which will grow progressively larger and progressively less able to

gain employment. We have become only too well aware of the economic and social problems of unemployment at the present time; we now have to ask ourselves what the situation will be like in five, or even ten year's time, for this is when those pupils whose work in the infant school we described at the beginning of Chapter 1 will be reaching the marketplace of the labour market. It is now that we need to think through the technological revolution of the present in order to prepare them — and ourselves — for that world. To do this we shall need to arrive at a clearer understanding of what we have called the Information Revolution: the product of a combination, as we have seen, of developments in computers and telecommunications. The new products in the High Street stores of which we spoke earlier are the results of the dramatic fall in the cost of computer equipment, which has been accompanied by a matching continual increase in performance capacity. A rule of thumb formula developed by some of those in the industry is that if you double the money that you spend on a computer system, you increase its performance potential tenfold. Writing in a special issue of the journal of the Albertan Teachers' Association devoted to the topic of computers in education, Kimon Valaskakis of the University of Montreal pursues a startling analogy:

> The increase in the performance – cost ratio has been so great since 1975 that some analysts suggest that a comparative development in the automobile industry would have allowed us to buy a Rolls-Royce Corniche today for five dollars (instead of the 120,000 dollars which is its list price). Alternatively, had that performance cost-ratio been applicable to aviation we could fly across the Atlantic on a 60,000 m.p.h. Concorde carrying 10,000 seats for five cents![8]

Put this vast amount of computer power, and therefore the power to access information in vast quantities speedily and accurately, alongside the other, comparable revolution that has been going on in telecommunications with the development of new communications systems such as cable distribution, satellite distribution, electronic mailing and banking, and fibre optics, and we have available to us what has been described as the electronic highway, 'an informational superhighway, as it were, spanning the globe and transmitting knowledge and data at the speed of light'.[9]

The impact of all this on education is likely to be two-fold: it points to the need to explore new curriculum content in order to give the student an understanding and mastery of the society that he will live in and, equally, it points (as we have already suggested) to the need to adapt and change educational methods themselves. How to do this and how to prepare future adults for a world in which the main area of expansion will be in the information industries, with the most probable occupation of future adults being in some way or another as information workers, is the current educational challenge. We hope in the remainder of this book to provide some guidelines as to how we may go about this.

3

New Things in New Ways!

Microcomputers are still novelties even in the schools that possess them. It is true that the numbers have been increasing very rapidly, partly because of Government assistance in purchase both for primary and secondary schools. However, large numbers of secondary schools will possess only one example of a first generation micro. At the time of writing, it seems as if it may be a considerable time yet before anything like a substantial proportion of schools are linked to such a national data-base such as Prestel. There are more schools probably with access to local data-banks, run by local authorities or local colleges, on a time-sharing basis.

It is easy, then, for the micro to become the prerequisite of one department in a school — commonly, and solely for historical reasons, the mathematics or science departments. It is quite common for computer studies to be an offshoot of a maths department.

This 'subject' has been growing, as one might expect, in recent years. However, it has not been growing as fast as some of its proponents have hoped. Certainly, a school which offers computer studies at 'O' level or for CSE is likely to attract fairly small groups of pupils to the option. The subject is not readily acceptable for higher education nor well understood by employers who, in the main, tend to prefer to do their own training. The subject, at worst, can be the province of a few and encourage the spending of a good deal of time on programming. Such a course will make a lot of use of the school micro and meanwhile the majority of pupils will get very little opportunity to handle the machine, let alone think about the implications of the revolution through which we are all living.

It is, of course, a major part of the argument of this book that all our children need to spend time in considering what is happening in our society and in developing the skills that will enable them to live a full and human life in the kind of world discussed in the previous chapter.

To engage in this task, as teachers in the humanities, is not so much to think about computers but about education. The tool, the very flexible tool, that is the computer will find its natural place in our curriculum if we, for our part, get the fundamentals right.

Certainly, it is not hard to see already some of the consequences of inadequate *educational* thought, not only in some computer studies courses but also in the materials being commercially produced in growing quantities for this new market. A substantial catalogue from a distributor, before us now, not surprisingly has a majority of programs in the field of maths and science. These are either drills ('Put in the Signs'; 'Tables', etc.) or tutorials on screen (a program teaching the principle of electric current). It is also not surprising to find that those few programs that are in our area of the curriculum are much the same — spelling drills, word games at the level of a simple crossword, learning the alphabet, sequencing exercises and so on. Anyone might be forgiven for thinking that a pencil and a piece of paper would be cheaper if such banal activities are needed in any classroom. It seems a silly waste of a complex and expensive machine. Of course, a micro will conduct a quiz or present information in an amusing, friendly and even vivid way. It will even act as a calculator, though a calculator is cheaper and more efficient at its particular tasks. What we need to ask always is whether the tasks we ask a computer to perform are worth doing in the first place. The modern proverb — garbage in, garbage out — applies to education just as much as to any other use of the computer.

The Nature of the Machine

If we are to think profitably about the place a microcomputer can take in our curriculum, we do need to think both about the curriculum and about the nature of the machine itself. If we understand the properties of the computer, we are better equipped to understand the part it might play in developing the kind of teaching that we and our pupils know we need.

The common-sense definition of a computer is that it is a machine for processing quantities of information. In their useful handbook *School Microcomputers: Uses and Management*[1] – Minicomputer Uses in Secondary Education (MUSE) list the following seven uses of the computer:

1. Learning by computer
2. Information retrieval
3. Text editing and/or word processing
4. Learning about computers
5. Administration, using the computer
6. Control technology — i.e. controlling the movements of other machines
7. Associated technology — e.g. viewdata and teletext, and other special purpose devices.

In all these uses, the computer is engaged in processing information — sorting it and presenting it. The computer that controls the robot has been fed with detailed information about the mechanical process the robot is to carry out. Administration requires that the computer is fed with the data on which to base decision taking. In the classroom, again, we find the computer used as an information processor, though to say this is to say nothing about whether the information or the processing is of educational value. The prior question must always be about the classroom task and whether it can be helped by utilizing the particular strengths of a computer.

We believe that the computer has certain advantages as an information processor. It is very fast, it is very accurate in its handling of the information humans have provided and, as technical development proceeds apace, it can hold ever larger quantities of data.

However, it is a laborious process programming any computer. Take, for example, the set of programs used by banks to check our accounts, to register our transactions and to print out at intervals our statements. It took years to write the programs so as to ensure that they always worked efficiently and accurately for the very large numbers of bank customers, large and small, and met their differing requirements. The time and effort needed to write the necessary programs was worth it to the bank because of the savings in time and labour and money that follow its use. It takes as long to write an educationally valueless program as one that meets the real needs of children learning in classrooms. So, the first criterion must always be educational quality.

As most people know, computers came into existence in order to deal quickly with numbers. The first computers were cumbersome calculating machines. Indeed, many are still performing such functions in industry and commerce. But computers are by no means limited to the manipulation of numbers in spite of their basis in binary mathematics. Modern computer languages enable us to use this binary system to encode any procedure that involves the processing of symbols. In a computer a binary number can represent itself. It can also represent a number in the decimal or any other number system; it can represent an instruction, a letter, or even a complete word.

In 1937, that extraordinary mathematical genius, Alan Turing, wrote a paper[2] which described what has since been known as a Turing machine. It was a theoretical account not, at that date, a blueprint for any kind of electric or electronic machine. What Turing showed was that, in theory, a machine could be made to carry out any procedure provided that the procedure was, in essence, computational and precisely defined. He used the term 'computational' here to cover any kind of symbolic processing (as described above) as opposed to, for example, such processes as standing for election or playing a musical instrument. If Turing was right, it became clear to his colleagues that it should be possible to build an almost infinite number of machines. Each Turing machine would embody the process it carried out. The step beyond this seminal paper in 1937 was to envisage the construction of a machine capable of carrying out whatever procedure it was instructed to carry out — a Universal Turing Machine, in fact.

That is just what we mean by a computer — a Universal Turing Machine able to carry out whatever we program it to do. We talked earlier about the seemingly obvious fact that a computer, like any machine, is a device with an input in order to get an output. This description seems less trivial when we appreciate that part of the input to a computer is, in effect, a description of the machine we want it to become, at any particular time. Before we program it a computer is an incomplete machine with only the potential to perform tasks. When we program it, it then becomes a machine to do what we want. The quality, then, of the output is the quality of the input. A trivial input yields a trivial output. The computer will feed back to us the quality of our educational thinking.

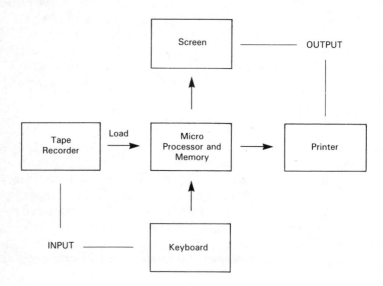

Input and Output to a Computer

It is not, incidentally, very important for us, as teachers, to know much about the actual workings of the machine. What we need to understand is the principle of the computer and something of the way in which programs are devised and constructed. The diagram shows broadly what is involved. The program that we input into the device we call a computer does two things. It gives the machine its instructions and also gives it the information it needs to carry out the instructions. It is not the function of this book to discuss how programs are written. The modern micro is likely to be accompanied by a comprehensive manual that will do more than just explain the bare workings of a keyboard. The manual will say a good deal about the ways in which programs are written and about the 'language' that a particular machine understands (BASIC in most educational micros). In addition, there are many books on the market to help anyone who wants to find out how to write programs and a lot of help can be gained from teacher organizations like MUSE and MAPE as well as User Groups for the enthusiasts. It is enough to appreciate at this stage that a program is initially based on a clear understanding of what is wanted and the detailed steps needed to arrive at the destination or destinations. Such a specification will probably look like a fairly complex flow diagram or branching diagram showing all the logical connections and alternative paths. It is in the thinking out of aims and how to move towards those aims that is found the educational thinking. The programmer translates the specification into the language of the machine as elegantly as possible.

The pioneers of computers were powerfully struck by the ability of the machine to process information. It is not surprising that educationists, when they began to think about the computer in the classroom, were influenced by the uses they saw in industry and commerce as well as their own previous experience of machines as aids to learning. So they tended to think of the classroom tasks that seemed to lend themselves to automation. The trouble is that to look for processes to fit the machine is not really to think about the processes themselves but rather to rationalize them.

Nowhere is this more obvious than in the use of the computer for drills and for revised versions of programmed learning. It is often argued that a major advantage of the micro in education is that it enables instruction to be individualized. Programs can be written or readily adapted for the needs of individual children. A teacher, once a problem has been diagnosed and a program found or devised to correct the problem, is freed to tackle those educational tasks that need the human touch. Indeed, some enthusiasts for the electronic future have been so excited by this vision of every pupil learning at his or her own pace that they have seen a future in which schools are no longer needed. Children learn at the home terminal. This is not quite the de-schooling envisaged by Ilich; it would perhaps turn out more like the Azimov short story where the children have to escape from the computer lesson in the locked house to find a wonder in sky and cloud and rain. This dream is also a harking back to the failed dreams of programmed learning. This time we have a better machine!

As recently as October 1978, Philip Venning wrote in *The Times Educational Supplement*:

> Indeed, the new technology may have an effect on schooling itself. Programmed learning may suddenly find a new acceptability in the home as the consumer market is increasingly flooded with cheap do-it-yourself learning toys, games and gadgets; while, in the long term, as industry dispenses with labour, public services such as education may be expanded substantially and class sizes of half a dozen might become quite normal.[3]

This article was reprinted as the major contribution on education in the highly influential *The Microelectronics Revolution*, edited by Tom Forester (Blackwell, 1980) with the support of the Department of Industry.

Historical ironies are catching up with us on an exponential curve. To anyone writing, like the present authors, early in 1983, such a dream of a reduced teaching force remotely supervising small groups of children in front of keyboards and screens is more like a nightmare. But Venning is right in talking about the computer toys in the High Street shops. They are with us almost in their hundreds — though evidence is beginning to appear that the novelty of some games, at least, is beginning to pall. The Space Invader tables in the pubs are not always occupied; sales of traditional toys are not entirely eroded. But among the computer packages in the shops are a number of so-called educational offerings — inefficient old ways of learning spelling or tables dressed up on talking machines together with a plethora of valueless quizzes and aids to rote learning, if any learning at all.

However, it is a mistake to ignore what is appearing in the High Street shops. These offerings represent a computerized version of the cram books that have been with us for too long already, but they do indicate yet again the gap between what is now educationally possible and the resistance to change that has so often anchored new technology in traditional pedagogy. Nevertheless, some of these toys are early efforts at what will soon be done well. We are not far away from the talking interactive computer, nor from the talking and *listening* interactive computer. (However, we do not share Christopher Evans's image in *The Mighty Micro*[4] of the future in education: children being educated on screen at home.)

There are, indeed, dangers ahead. Technology, not for the first time, is moving ahead of some political and much educational thinking. We have already noted, with programmed learning, the danger of putting this new wine in that or any other old bottle. Of course, there are instructional situations where programmed learning is useful and efficient. Industry has long known that certain techniques or procedures can best be taught in such a way. No doubt there are some classroom procedures which can be more efficiently and pleasantly learnt through the short steps of programmed learning with its reinforcement of the right answers. The trouble has been that behaviourists have taken this model of step-by-step learning with each step reinforced as a model for all learning. We are no longer blinkered in our vision of children by the old Skinnerian certainties. We know there are still many unanswered questions about how children learn and no generally accepted unifying theory. We do, though, as educationists, have some idea of the teaching procedures that work in particular contexts.

Yet Learning Theory dies hard. It is still the orthodoxy on a number of teaching training courses and our schools are full of teachers who were reared on operant conditioning — although most have probably discarded the rigours of the theory faced with the practice that is by no means so simple and tidy. Of course, as we have said, there are occasions when children do learn better when rewarded for right answers. All we wish to stress here is that how any of us see the way in which children learn must affect how we see the potential of the computer in the classroom.

If our model of learning is basically that of operant conditioning then, of course, we shall see the computer as offering a considerable enhancement of programmed learning. This enhancement, it is argued, comes about in two ways:

1. A greatly improved routing system through the material to be taught; and
2. Through the user-friendly approach to programming, the simulation of a rewarding conversation between machine and pupil.

Here is an example:

Machine	*Pupil*
Words that end in Y generally form their plural by changing the Y to I and adding ES. Thus TRY becomes TRIES, PRY becomes PRIES, and so on. Why don't you try one?	
What is the plural of SKY?	SKYS
No, remember the rule about words that end in Y.	
Now, what is the plural of SKY?	SKYES
No, you have the idea but you misspelled the answer.	
Try again. What is the plural of SKY?	SKIES
There you got it. Here's another one.	

And so on! Not the brightest of pupils, perhaps, though seemingly he could cope with reading the messages on the screen. The extract also illustrates quite clearly what is meant, in the jargon, by 'user-friendly'.

Now this kind of program, whatever one thinks of its value, does not make full advantage of the potential of the machine. The tracking is more sophisticated than on the old programmed learning machine and it is possible to brighten up the screens with graphics and colour. But does not experience tell us that children soon become bored with such material? The praise from the screen has a diminishing return in attention or the child begins to sus out the machine. Getting the answer wrong can be as much fun as getting it right — perhaps more! More seriously, this kind of program provides no opportunity for the transfer of any learning to any kind of meaningful context. It is as open to objection as any old-fashioned spelling book or word list, and even more careless. Since when was *pries* a plural? Secondly, the program assumes the isolation of the child who is cut off from any fruitful discussion with his peers.

In our view, then, the Learning Theory model for computer use is simplistic and flawed. It takes for granted that education is the acquisition of facts or concepts treated as facts. It is Gradgrind Redivivus and, like the offerings of that utilitarian, it can still be found lurking in some of the current demands for standards or a 'return to basics'. At another level, Mastermind equals Standards! Of course, what this model of learning cannot do is to take into account the exploration of ideas and feelings. It is a barrier to questioning and ignores personal experience as the foundation for growth. It lacks any sense of how the whole person is involved in real learning.

If this is so, then, either the computer is as limited as the old programmed learning or there is a greater potential than such theorists have understood. If we are to make effective use of the machine, then we need to look closely at what we believe to be the means whereby we can best achieve those goals. What is the nature of the enquiry? What are the best means for our pupils to discover a problem and move towards its solution? If a computer program offers us the means to achieve our educational goals then to the computer program we should turn. The decision we take is exactly on the same grounds as a decision to use a book or a film or tape.

We need, therefore, always to be clear in our minds about what a particular program has to offer. It is thus helpful, in general terms, to be aware of the various ways in which a computer can be used. A useful way of looking at the role of the computer in education can be found in Nick Rushby's *An Introduction to Educational Computing.*[5] He makes use of four 'educational paradigms' devised by a group at the University of East Anglia to assist exploration of the educational potential of the computer. They are:

1. *Instructional*: covering programmed learning, drills, tests, etc.
2. *Revelatory*: problem solving, concept teaching, etc.
3. *Conjectural*: model building, exploring, etc.
4. *Emancipatory*: freeing both teacher and pupil to concentrate on essentials.

The fourth paradigm can appear in association with any of the other three. We look now at some of the possibilities under these headings.

The Instructional Paradigm

We have already seen a 'spelling lesson'. He is another example quoted approvingly in Christine Doerr's *Microcomputers and the 3 Rs*:

Machine	*Pupil*
Hello, what is your name?	Chris
Chris, today we are going to talk about the first three Presidents of the United States. Of course, you know who the first President was, don't you, Chris?	Yes
Tell me his last name.	Washington

> That's right. In 1789, George Washington was elected President
> by the unanimous vote of the State electors. John Adams was his Vice-
> President for both terms (1789 – 1796).

Would not Chris have problems with the language used here? Could he read
and understand 'unanimous'? Who are the State electors? What is a 'term'?
After much more, Chris has to face a quiz — needless to say, not one that involves any understanding of the concepts implicitly present in the information
given:

Machine	*Pupil*
OK Chris, now I'm going to ask you some questions.	
A. Who was elected President in 1796?	
1. George Washington	
2. John Adams	
3. Abraham Lincoln	
Type the number of the correct answer.	3
No. Lincoln was President from 1860 – 65. Try again.	1
No. Washington declined nomination for a third term.	
The answer is John Adams.	

Poor Chris! This is almost a classic example of the so-called comprehension
question that can be answered by guesswork without reading a word of the
text. Are we sure, though, that there will not be a flood in Britain of such
mindless programs masquerading as educational? We have already noted the
poverty-stricken nature of those to be found in the shops. Current publishers'
catalogues are not wholly reassuring. Many programs seem to do little beyond
purvey information, albeit graphically, or test. Children are, of course,
fascinated by what they see on VDUs — for a while anyway. Using the
keyboard in response to a screen message seems to be motivating — again for
a time. So vacuous CAL (Computer Assisted Learning) programs seem initially to be successful.

    Rushby comments: 'The concept of using the computer to guide students
through structured course materials is based on the assumption that the majority of students should follow one of a small number of paths.' The first
generation of microcomputers to become widely available for schools had
limited memory capacity (commonly 16K) and this, in turn, limited the scope
of the programs that could be written for them. The current generation has at
least twice the capacity with the potential for building on. In a few years' time,
microcomputers will be in the shops at low prices with memories of 64K or
more. No doubt behavioural psychologists will be able to devise even more
complex instructional mazes for student rats and pigeons. The educational
world, however, will have the computer capacity to permit a far more imaginative approach to the use of the machines in the classroom. Already, the 'state

of the art' permits a far more interesting and stimulating use of language, graphics and interaction than we have seen so far.

Of course, one avenue that is open to us is the use of the computer for rather more satisfactory modes of testing and individual teaching. As early as 1962, advocates of CAL were contemplating the ease of automation, the time saving and the gains in classroom management. More importantly, psychologists were noting the discovery that students (and, interestingly, patients in hospital clinics) found it was easier and less personally embarrassing to talk to the machine than to a human being. Indeed, there is good evidence now of the value of well-constructed programs for use in special and remedial education. As always, when the program works well and leads to educational gains this is because the prior educational thinking was sound.

The Revelatory Paradigm

Rushby defines this model as follows:

> Whereas in the instructional form the computer is used to present the subject material, to monitor the student's responses and to control his progress through the course module, in revelatory Computer Assisted Learning (CAL), the computer acts as a mediator between the student and a hidden module of some real life situation.

There are a number of situations where this mode can be fully justified in terms of objectives and instructional context. For example, it is common practice to train scientists and technicians on the behaviour of nuclear reactors through simulations. A highly structured program leads the student through a simulation of actual conditions. After all, it would be rather dangerous to experiment with the real thing! Similarly, war games can be played through a computer. At school level, simulations can be used to lead students through a historical battle or a voyage of exploration so that they can gain some experience of the kind of decision taking involved at the time. There are now a number of good scientific programs in this mode — especially where experimental work is not possible in the normal school laboratory. Students can discover through a computer program with vivid graphics something about such processes as, on the one hand, genetic change and, on the other, the slow processes of geological change. Where other media are passive, such programs can offer the student a measure of interaction and rather more of a sense of discovery. Similarly, in hospitals we find computer simulations being used to take students through the diagnostic process.

Of course, in all such programs, the student is being led to a predetermined conclusion, the discovery of something already known. Even so, there are clear uses for the mode and later chapters will suggest further possibilities in the Humanities. At this stage of the discussion, two examples may suffice.

The Revelatory Paradigm might well be the right model for a computer program on oil pollution and how it develops and is countered. Students could be taken through a simulation of an actual example. Similarly, this seems to be a helpful model for a study of population problems, using graphs and population pyramids to assist the student to understand how predictions are made and how they are changed by changing birth rates. A third example, already in school use, is a computer program on diets. The student can create menus and the computer will provide an analysis of nutritional value.

The model still largely presupposes the individual learner — though small group discussion is often helpful in tackling such programs. The material (information) is structured. In the instructional model, the machine quizzes the student. In this model, the student must question the machine or inform the machine of decisions to take one course rather than another. The educational context has widened.

The Conjectural Paradigm

We have already met in Chapter 1 an example of this model. The young historians by questioning the census data were able to use the information they obtained to build up their own model of historical change. The computer had become a tool very much in the control of the students, doing the chores for them, freeing them to develop effective hypotheses.

A rather different example of this model would be the simulation where there are no right answers. Suppose a group of students wants to look at a planning problem — a simulation, perhaps, of a motorway enquiry. In real life, a great deal depends in such cases on the information that is made available — traffic flows, land use and requirements, environmental impact, etc. Many of these factors can be analysed in terms of a cost – benefit analysis. What a good computer program can do is to provide a data-bank of information relevant to the simulation on which the parties can draw as they enact the enquiry. We shall see, in a later example on data-banks, a whole series of programs that help students to clarify their own thinking about careers.

It is our view that this model offers the most potential for humanities teaching which, after all, has as its purpose helping students to make sense of their lives and the life of their community as best they may. It is not an area of study much given to right answers but it is an area of study that profits enormously when students are taught how to question and how to find out for themselves.

There are other advantages in this use of the computer as provider of information on which to base conjectures and hypotheses. There is no doubt that the kind of work we have been briefly describing can only be done in groups. The young historians of Chapter 1 worked through discussion. They had to decide what they wanted to know and how to 'interrogate' the computer. They had to discuss the information they acquired and what it implied. Our motor-way enquiry clearly involves discussion and debate. It also involves decisions about the use of the computer. The whole program is designed to lead towards a decision. Of course, it is entirely possible to organize group activities, without computers, that involve discussion and decision taking. There are adventure games that work without a computer (and adventure games also in-volve talking and deciding). What the computer program can do is to extend the range of possibilities for such educationally valuable activities and, to some extent, extend the motivation of the students. (For further discussion of these issues see Chapter 6.)

The Emancipatory Paradigm

Rushby's final model is of a different order. We can find examples in all the other three modes where the computer is used in order to free a student to con-centrate on what is the more important aspect of a particular learning process. The machine can tackle informational chores for us — much as a pocket calculator does. It can rapidly sort information for us into the form in which we require it. It can set up for us a situation that makes discussion possible. Virtually all the examples quoted in the sections on both Revelatory and Conjectural Paradigms show the computer also emancipating the students from chores of one kind or another.

To Summarize

All of Rushby's modes have their uses in the classroom. All have potential dangers. In the instructional mode the computer is a patient, if rather limited, tutor, sometimes a rather trivial and boring one. In the revelatory mode, the computer mediates between the student and a model contained in the program which the student will be led to discover. All depends on the quality of the model. In the conjectural mode, the students create their own hypotheses on the basis of the information they can retrieve from the machine. The success of such programs depends very much on the skill of the programmer in antici-pating the information that students will want and the form in which they will want it.

Always, the computer is no more than an aid. Whether we use it, or how we use it, depends always on our own understanding of how pupils learn and our own assessment of whether and how this machine can help us achieve our goals.

We conclude this chapter (before we look in some detail at various aspects of the humanities curriculum) with two further thoughts: an experiment, and a comment on education from a distinguished scientist that seems to us to apply to more than the teaching of science in our schools and colleges.

The Experiment

Many teachers, as we have seen, have argued that the computer enables them to exercise greater control over the learning process. Our argument is that this is a misuse of the machine, for the machine can more effectively be used to help students make their own choices, conduct their own experiments. It is much safer making an unwise decision on a computer than in real life! What is more there is good evidence to show that procedures controlled by students are more effective in teaching. J. R. Hartley of the Computer Based Learning Unit at Leeds University, devised an experiment to look at the comprehension of texts. The material was mathematical but this, in itself, does not seem to be significant. Sixty students took part and were randomly divided into three groups. Each group was presented with the same passage. Group 1 was told that the text was being tested for readability and they were asked to note words of more than six letters in length or which seemed hard to spell. Group 2 answered questions at various points in the text which asked for paraphrasing of the material. Group 3 also had questions as they read, but these asked for examples of the ideas being discussed.

Afterwards all students were given three tests: a free-recall, a cued recall and a comprehension test. Groups 2 and 3 did much better than Group 1 on these tests. Answers tended for them to be in sentences, for Group 1 in words or short phrases. Group 2 did best on free-recall; Group 3 on the comprehension test. Further, students with a good deal of mathematical experience and knowledge did best on cued recall and comprehension. The less experienced benefited most from the invitation to construct examples. In other words, those students who made the text for them into a learning experience, related the concepts as far as possible to their own experience: they were taking control themselves of the material. Other experiments confirmed these findings and the large individual differences between the students. Hartley argues, in conclusion, that: 'the importance of the perceptions and knowledge which each individual student brings to the task (and which is often unknown to the teacher) argue for increased learner control provided that supporting advice can be obtained.'[7]

The Scientist

In *The Times Educational Supplement* of 10 September 1982, Sir Hermann Bondi laments much in the current state of science education. He points out that science is inescapably an important part of our culture. Yet the assumption is generally made that science courses need to have a vocational slant. 'To this end, it has been thought essential that students are fed a heavy diet based on the results of scientific research.'[8]

We can recognize some parallels in the humanities. The courses in schools are not vocational in the same sense, but, nevertheless, there are equivalent beliefs, only too often, in the importance of the heavy diet.

Sir Hermann goes on to say:

> I believe that the most fascinating thing about science is its methods and its ways of working . . . To me, the very essence of science is its questioning nature, its inherent uncertainty, its utter dependence on constant and intense communication. I believe that what is fascinating about science is not the things we think we know, but the doubts about what we know, how we hope to resolve at least some of those doubts. Thus progress is perhaps the most intensely human of all activities. Nothing in science matters until it is discussed with others, nothing in science is remotely real until it is published, nothing in science is significant unless it has influenced others.

The article goes on to consider the implications of this vision of the pursuit of science for teaching. What are the needs of potential young scientists for an understanding of how to communicate? 'In science, we do not offer facts, we offer a method of co-operation'. Yet, Sir Hermann notes, so much of science teaching is the teaching of facts, the teaching of certainties. No wonder, he observes, that the popular view of science is of a kind of wizardry. By failing to convey the sense of exploration, of finding a way through doubts and uncertainties, we fail to convey any appreciation of the place of science in our culture:

> Science offers tremendous opportunities for use in general education, opportunities that we do not take advantage of . . . My plea, therefore, is that we make science much more attractive to much larger numbers of people, by teaching it as it really is, as a human endeavour in which the effort and steps that turn out to be unsuccessful enormously outnumber those that are successful. . . . We will then have in our society more people who realise what kind of questions you can ask in science and what kind of answers you can expect. . . . We have got to get away from the concept of teaching science as a subject with definite results.

What has this to do with a discussion of the potential of the computer in humanities courses? First of all, much of what Sir Hermann Bondi says about science is true of any form of human intellectual endeavour. The science he loves is the science of both physicist and historian, of both chemist and geographer, of both biologist and student of language. Education is not the purveying of facts in little packages; it is learning how to ask questions and seek answers.

It has been the argument of this chapter that the computer can provide us with a most valuable tool with which to encourage the development of this questioning, this 'constant and intense communication'. The machine is neutral, incomplete. We can enlist it in the service of our latter-day Gradgrinds and use it to fill the little vessels with facts. We can also enlist it in the cause of truly human endeavour, in 'co-operation and communication'.

In the remainder of this book, we turn to look in greater detail at how, in the humanities, we can make our contribution to developing that spirit of enquiry so that our young people are better equipped to take control over their own lives and to cope with the continuing pace of change in a dangerous world.

4

Why we Need to Adapt

In their interesting book of speculations on the implications of the Information Revolution for social change, *Gutenberg Two*, Godfrey *et al* have an interesting essay on education in which they make a very strong case for computer-assisted learning to deal with the routine elements in any syllabus:

> The creative teacher will be delighted to see 80% of the rote aspects of any discipline adapted for presentation by this methodology for many reasons. First of all, it forces one to examine the content of what is being taught . . . Secondly, one must seriously examine one's assumptions about how the material might best be presented . . . Suppose one needn't worry about holding up the entire class for half an hour while Paul grasps the second law of thermodynamics; suppose it doesn't matter if he needs fifteen examples instead of two? Do you have fifteen? Why didn't the first fourteen work? Perhaps what is needed is more drama, or humour, or a game context?[1]

They go on to make the point that the invention of moveable type and the development of printing ('Gutenberg One') led to the development of the 'schoolroom', 'an appendage of a library, a room in which books can be distributed, collected and stored';Gutenberg *Two* requires no such appendage. Theoretically, in computer-assisted learning contexts with every student working on an individualized program specifically catering for his needs and enabling him to work at his own pace and obtain instant and personalized information about his progress, there is no reason why the student should not obtain skills and knowledge without ever leaving his home. Indeed, many of the more innovative minds concerned at present with the use of computers in learning see the potential of the home market as being considerable. Some would strongly argue the virtues of this as a means of liberating the student from the tyranny of the 'schoolroom', the subordination of the student to the mind and talents (or otherwise) of the schoolmaster. From some points of view this can be seen as an essentially progressivist stance, one well in line with the thinking of radical educators such as Illich and Holt. Godfrey concludes his analysis thus:

> Education has existed for a long time without serious competition, partly because of its social function and partly because of its high labour content;

competition is about to arrive . . . The educational system at the present . . . is the accepted and valued knowledge of the society. It is place-bound, time-bound and unused to competition or innovation. No other sector of society is more vulnerable to the new technologies. I will predict, however, that within the system (after an initial period of protest), terror will become the mother of adaptation, and although the formal structure will continue to shrink as the work week shortens, creative teachers will have tasks and opportunities that they had previously never even considered possible.

To this we would add that it is precisely because the impact of the Microelectronics and Information Revolution on society are so far-reaching that schools and teachers will also have to adapt, not just to survive as institutions, but in order to fit the young to take their place in the world of work and leisure as it is currently evolving. We discussed in Chapter 2 some of the aspects of the changing employment situation and its implications for the work of the schools.

The following figures will help to illustrate more precisely the changes that have taken place in the last few years in the organisation of workers into various sectors in the industrial sphere:

	% of the working population	
	1970	*1977*
Those engaged in manufacturing, agricultural, and construction industries. Gas, electricity and water services.	44.9	39.5
Service industries, including communications, distributive and professional services. National and local government.	47.4	52.8

(The remainder of the total working population is accounted for by employers or self-employed in each case.)

Later figures are not at present easily available but will certainly have been affected by the massive increase in unemployment which will have further affected the trend away from the manufacturing industries.

In the United States Porat[2] differentiates between service industries and those working in information supplying and using industries and shows that about 60% of this part of the labour force was involved in the information handling side and the remaining 40% in the other services. There is every reason to suppose that similar figures could be extrapolated for the other countries shown in the graph above.

This becomes especially important when we consider the impact of the Information Revolution and its social effects. It has been argued that one of the results of the original Industrial Revolution was to lead to a de-skilling of the labour force. Craftsmen were replaced by mass methods of production; the satisfaction obtained by doing a job from beginning to end and of considering design features alongside the process of manufacture was lost as men (or 'hands') on the production line were engaged in low level and purely repetitive tasks. Jones[3] makes this point well:

> Broad areas of work in industrial society are characterised by an almost total lack of intrinsic reward. But leisure pursuits are also in many cases passive and uncreative, there being no widespread evidence that individuals use their leisure time as an effective compensation for the deprivations of work.

He quotes, tellingly, two accounts:

> The jobs being done by all of us out on the floor were identical, as far as I could see. We had a pile of stores vouchers, a register, an indelible pencil each. There were numbers in your register which tallied with the vouchers. You had to find the corresponding number, tick a space, turn the voucher from a pile on your right to one on your left. No talking, no contact, nothing — unless you counted trips to the bogs.

> Select the gear box, lift it with the hoist and stick it into the hole in the middle of the engine. It's quicker if you do it without the hoist. But watch your back. Screw down the top bolts and secure the gear box to the engine . . . There are worse jobs. On the struts for example — installing the suspension units, a quarter of a hundredweight at a time. Bending down all day. Men have had haemorrhages from working on the struts. So they share the job around. There's another bad job on the trim lines — installing the headlamps. Sat on a little trolley with wheels on. Your head underneath the wheel arches. Being pushed along by the line.

And comments: 'Do we have any right to lament the loss of jobs like these?'

Interestingly a possible result of the increased use of microcomputers in the fast-growing information sector of industry may be to restore some of the sense of job satisfaction lost in the first Industrial Revolution. It is true that, as electronics get progressively more dependent upon printed circuit boards and on the chip itself as a means of carrying electrical information, the work of the erstwhile electrical engineer (or at any rate that of the repair man) will become just a matter of plugging in a new board or chip. But, by contrast, as Evans points out (*op.cit.*, p.165) in the information handling positions, which (as we have seen) are likely to grow, much more job satisfaction may be expected. Thus in the newspaper industry the job of the compositor who has neither interest in nor control over the words he sets up in type may disappear for through computerized type-setting it is possible for the journalist to key in copy directly to the computer and directly to control layout and typesetting. The same applies to industries such as that of travel. Instead of being a mere filler-in and transmitter of information through forms, the clerk in the High

Street office will be able to communicate directly with airlines and form an immediate link between the client and the services the client seeks to avail himself of. That is, of course, until the development of systems such as Prestel make the accessibility of news and travel booking facilities in one's own home a matter of everyday life so that the notion of the consumer as providing services to himself on a self-help basis (already well established in the supermarket and self-service points such as bank cash points and petrol stations) becomes the norm. (It is commonly said that the office jobs that remain will be more interesting. But there are complaints about much current VDU work — screen reading, warehouses, etc. — complaints of boredom, eyestrain and exploitation. We should not be unduly optimistic that exploitation will be ended by the chip.)

All of this has considerable implications for what we are doing in the schools.

If the clerk behind the desk in the travel agency is to take on these responsibilities; if we, the bank customers, are to take over more of the responsibility for running our own accounts without the mediation of the teller between our account and ourselves; if we are going to be able to access our own choice of news from the sources that provide the news without having it mediated to us by journalists; then the necessity of helping students acquire high-order thinking skills becomes paramount. Up to now it has been perfectly acceptable for schools to *instruct* pupils — that is, to pass on knowledge to them (to a large extent) to tell them what to think. It has been well said, for example, that much of the so-called 'enquiry method' is actually 'discovery method', providing that the student discovers what the teacher intends him to discover. (See much of the programme in Nuffield Science for example.) But in the age created by the Information Revolution this will be insufficient since the client will inevitably be put much more in the position of being also a manager. This suggests that along with the skills of collaborating and getting on with one another (important in a more leisured society) we shall have to be teaching managerial skills. Potentially the opportunity is with us today for more people to take active control over their own lives than ever before — and this means mere passive, that is receptive, learning will be insufficient to meet the needs of a rapidly-changing society. All of the above presupposes, of course, important social changes that will need to go along with the effects of the Information Revolution. The social studies curriculum must be subject to constant and careful scrutiny to ensure that it explores these social changes accompanying the microelectronics revolution. It is not enough just to utilize the new technology in teaching.

Yet, even without the demands of the Information Revolution to cope with, the educational system shows itself very slow to change and develop to meet the changed demands of an industrial situation. In 1981 and 1982 the National Association for the Teaching of English held, along with the Careers Research and Advisory Centre (CRAC), a series of conferences looking at communication skills needed in industry by young people entering employment. The proceedings of these conferences were published under the title *English, Communication Skills and the Needs of People in Industry*[4], which is introduced thus:

> The poor language performance of young people — particularly school leavers — entering employment is a constant complaint of employers. What are these complaints? Are they true? *What are the actual language demands made on young people going into jobs?* How should schools, colleges and employers assist young people to communicate effectively and efficiently? (our italics)

The conferences, in seeking answers to these questions, drew upon a wealth of experience from educationists and industrialists, and, in particular, had the opportunity of considering the evidence available from Local Education Authority working parties seeking to investigate these questions. The conclusions they, and the conferences, came to were startlingly similar. For example, there is now abundant evidence that young people going into their first jobs do not need a great deal of skill in writing (though this may be required later) but abilities in reading, and (above all) in talking and listening are of fundamental importance. Studies in two LEAs as different as Essex and Coventry came up with very similar conclusions and placed the ability to communicate orally, especially in different kinds of social situation, very high in their order of priorities. The Coventry report makes an interesting point in respect of this:

> In schools, it is normally the adults who initiate conversations; but, in employment, it appeared that the manager is not likely to speak to an apprentice. If the apprentice wishes to speak to the manager, it is the apprentice who must begin the conversation. Similarly, there is little social talk between foreman and apprentice. All the previous experience of a school leaver has been that the main function of talk is to establish and maintain relationships; given that assumption, young workers in many firms presumably take the unspoken messages of their work-place to indicate that certain kinds of relationship are ruled out totally. And yet, at the same time, there are demands, sometimes in the same firms, that the apprentice should be able to take an active role in problem-solving discussion teams. There is a dissonance here which generally remains inexplicit.[5]

Levi in *Preventing Work Stress* makes a valuable and cognate point:

> One of the great advantages of working life is that it creates the social context for contact and collaboration with other human beings. These are basic human needs. Accordingly, conversation and contact between employees should be made a necessary part of the production process instead of being eliminated. Whenever possible, work should be planned in such a way that

its various components could be allocated to relatively small groups of say four to eight people. Speech and eye contact and collaboration among the group should be encouraged. If these turn out to be impossible for practical reasons, human contact should be facilitated at least during the rest pauses, and opportunities for friendly contact with supervisors and managers should be promoted.[6]

It seems likely that the pressures suggested in the above analysis will increase rather than diminish as a result of the direction industrial employment (and unemployment) will take as a consequence of the microelectronic revolution.

What, then, are the implications of all this for the classroom? It seems to us that some of the questions relating to industrial management and training raised above have a direct analogy with the management problems immediately involved when we introduce a microcomputer into the classroom. If we assume about thirty students in the class and, at the most, one microcomputer in each classroom, there are clearly important problems to be solved. How do we ensure that everyone gets an opportunity to work at the terminal? How do we usefully employ the other pupils? How do we provide some focus and integration for the work going on in the room as a whole? Perhaps Levi's solution of working in small groups in terms of industrial development strategy will provide us with the only possible answer to our classroom management problem, while, at the same time, enabling us to provide more of the education in and through talk that, we have seen, is already greatly needed in preparing students for the working world.

Jones (1980) has a useful check list of the management problems which 'should concern every teacher who intends using the microcomputer within a classroom'. These include:

- Where do you position the system within the classroom so as to cause the least disturbance yet give easy access to the user and 'in-view' supervision for the teacher?
- How do you ensure equal access by all pupils within the class?
- How do you ensure that the children receive maximum benefit from using it, with the minimum interference from the teacher?
- How do you 'manage' the software?
- How do you plan for the computer's impact on the children's other work?
- How do you ensure that careful records are kept of its use?
- How do you evaluate its use by the children?[7]

These and similar vital practical questions are further explored in Jones[8] and Chandler[9]. It is significant that both writers are looking at the questions from the standpoint of the primary school classroom. It may well be that teachers in such classrooms, well experienced as many of them are in having a number of related, but different, activities taking place simultaneously within the same clasroom space, are better placed than the traditional secondary school teacher to adapt to the management tactics that will be needed if we are to make the best use of the new technology in the classroom. Indeed, we shall see in a later chapter, the impact of the microprocessor in strengthening the already growing arguments for the breaking down of some of the traditional boundaries between disciplines in the humanities area of the curriculum. But, for a whole host of reasons, as Bernstein[10] among others has shown, such curriculum change is very difficult to implement at secondary school level.

One thing seems clear. The teacher intending to introduce the micro-computer into the classroom will have to evolve strategies of group work. Our own thinking and experience leads us to believe that the most likely solution will lie in the direction of the development of 'packages' of material with the computer program. The use of the computer to run programs will be simply one ingredient in a much more thoroughgoing collection of teaching materials that could include work-cards, conventional print materials, audio-visual resources and the like. The arguments for resource-based learning have been well rehearsed by now (see Taylor[11]) and we already know a great deal about the management of group work within the 'informal' classroom. The intelligent use of the microcomputer in the classroom is liable to provide a new impetus for such approaches which have suffered something of a decline in educational fashion since the '60s and early '70s. There does not appear to be any other equally convenient way of solving the managerial problems that Jones and others have pointed to. But it also seems, if the foregoing analysis has any validity, that it is precisely in group work for its own sake (not just adopted as a management strategy) that we shall be able to develop those skills that students will actually need in the world of work, skills such as the ability to co-operate and communicate with others through talking in a variety of social contexts, to solve problems, to explore the creative uses of the imagination. If we look at the evidence from the NATE/CRAC conferences and from the reports of the Essex and Coventry LEAs, we shall see that it is precisely those skills that they came to focus on as needed by young people in industry which are most likely to be developed by adapting the classroom environment to take account of the introduction of the microcomputer. This insistence upon the microcomputer as one resource among many, as only a part of the total learning package, and the emphasis we have placed upon the use of groups when pupils are working at the computer terminal seems to characterize all the best work of its kind that we described in Chapter 1. It is far removed from the approach to education which is still, to a large extent, being upheld by senior officials of the DES and by many of the examination boards, that is a view of education as mere 'knowledge peddling' with a stress upon the ability to recall predigested information. If the microcomputer is used solely as an instrument of 'instruction', if we see it primarily as a means of leading to individualized learning from pre-packaged programs, then we shall not have begun to realize its possibilities for promoting healthy change within the school and classroom. It is only when we recognize its potential for providing a powerful motivation and focus for group work, a means of developing talk and group interaction, generating the opportunity to try to solve problems rather than guess already predetermined solutions, that we shall really be making use of the microcomputer in a distinctively educational way and beginning to do more than we do at present to prepare our students to meet the real needs of the world at work. Watts (1979), in an important article, 'The Implications of School-Leaver Unemployment for Careers Education in Schools', points to some of the ways in which what goes on in schools needs to change:

> . . . a prime task of education will be to equip students with the skills, concepts and information they need to be able to define who they are, who they want to be, and what community needs they can help to meet. This will need to be a recurrent activity: in other words, people will return to educational institutions periodically through their lives to reorientate themselves as well as to acquire additional skills which they need in order to perform new roles. Careers education will become a central activity in a system of recurrent education . . . Rather than being concerned with slotting people into the pre-created jobs that exist (or do not exist) for them, it will be able to encourage and equip people, if necessary, to create their own work. [12]

In his contributions to the conferences already mentioned Watts took this thinking a stage further:

> It is arguable that only under the 'right to work' scenario will the traditional curriculum remain viable; even there, the opportunity for a more creative approach to the concept of 'work' has considerable curricular repercussions . . . What does seem clear . . . is that the traditional concepts of work that have dominated Britain since the Industrial Revolution are breaking down. Whether this becomes a destructive or creative force depends a great deal on whether as a society we are able to address ourselves to the basic issues it raises, and to perceive its opportunities. Schools have a crucial role to play here. Pupils leaving school in 1982 will still only be in their mid-thirties in the year 2001, and their attitudes will significantly determine society's capacity to grapple creatively with the profound processes of social change that seem to be taking place. [13]

If there is any truth at all in this analysis then the potential of the microcomputer for creative rather than passive models of learning in the classroom will be neglected at our peril.

It certainly has important implications for our understanding of what we are about even at the level of 'computer assisted instruction'. Sharples has pointed out some of the dangers that exist:

> Designers and users of CAI programs are already being lured by technology and the constraints of the curriculum into accepting inferior teacher substitutes, equipped with outmoded and incomplete principles of edu-

cation. No headmaster would welcome a teacher with a didactic and patronis-
ing style, knowledge confined to a single teaching scheme and poor ability to
meet the wide range of demands from pupils; market it as a 'microcomputer
teaching package' and every school wants one. [14]

   The kind of 'quiz' type programs masquerading as 'educational software' in
the High Street shops are a good example of the kind of thing being produced.
It is only when, by contrast, the education is in the process experienced by the
students rather than in the product to which they are subjected that real learning is likely to take place, or, at any rate, learning that has any relevance to the
complex needs of society identified and explored above. By contrast with the
more primitive kind of educational software for computer aided instruction
we may consider what Jones actually calls 'process skills'. While not denying
other kinds of learning that can be aided by the computer he places great stress
upon these also.

> In using the computer, individuals or small groups will be developing and
> practising many skills. They will be exposed to machines having the human
> attitudes of humour, warmth, criticism, stress, patience and praise. They
> will be given practice in skills so important in equipping them to cope with
> life, such as problem-solving skills, decision-making, and learning short-,
> medium-, and long-term consequences of decisions made. They will be given
> practice in divergent as well as convergent thinking skills, such as flexibility,
> fluency, originality, evaluating, hypothesising, as well as memory skills, with
> the benefits of a rapid feedback and correction. They will face both success
> and failure in a controlled environment and be taught to learn from failure
> and to develop the patience and care needed to succeed. Good subject-
> orientated programs have some of these skill developments contained within
> them — but it is up to the teacher to recognize and exploit them to the full;
> otherwise the computer . . . can be viewed as a rote-teaching, testing
> machine — and that would be a sad indictment of the teacher not the
> microcomputers. It could also be an indictment of *poor programs*. (author's
> emphasis) [15]

If we are able to devise and exploit programs that place a due emphasis upon
these 'process skills' the kinds of learning that Watts and others have
suggested is so important for the year 2001 will be greatly aided and
encouraged.

   To realize this potential in practice, of course, will need some model of computer education from which to operate, especially if we are to think adequately
in subject-based terms. Luckily a good deal of the necessary thinking has been
done at least in an embryo form by the team based at the College of St Mark
and St John concerned with Investigations into Teaching with Microcomputers as an Aid (the ITMA project) which has compiled a list to help the
teacher decide how the computer might be able to assist his teaching. The
following list (taken from Jones, 1981) [16] indicates their suggested applications

for education using computers that teachers might consider in planning a programme of works:

(a) Computer talents

    (i) speed
    (ii) graphics
    (iii) animation
    (iv) randomization
    (v) external device control
    (vi) timing control
    (vii) selective input

(b) Human 'attitudes'

    (i) humour
    (ii) warmth
    (iii) praise
    (iv) criticism
    (v) stress
    (vi) patience

(c) Styles or tactics

    (i) games
    (ii) simulation
    (iii) competition
    (iv) catalytic motivation
    (v) flexibility
    (vi) command structure
    (vii) management
    (viii) diagnostics
    (ix) programmed learning
    (x) environment control

(d) Activities

    (i) exercising
    (ii) role playing in environment
    (iii) investigation
    (iv) introduction to topic
    (v) extension or exposition of topic
    (vi) revision of topic
    (vii) problem-solving — strategic or tactical skills

(e) Styles of teaching

    (i) balance between machine/teacher/pupil
    (ii) open or planned progression
    (iii) use of program flexibility
    (iv) teacher's use of the program

As Jones aptly comments: 'There are so many permutations possible that no teacher could complain that their individual approach to class teaching would be impaired in any way — rather the opposite would be the effect, for the computer allows for so many more options to be made.'[17]

As we have seen, schools are always very slow to adapt to necessary change. It is our conviction that the investment nationally in the introduction of the microcomputer into schools alongside our growing understanding of the implications of the microelectronics revolution and the associated Information Revolution may provide the greatest stimulus yet to curriculum development within and across subject areas. How this might be worked out in detail in terms of specific areas of the curriculum is the subject of exploration in the chapters that follow.

5

Asking Questions;
Getting Answers

In this section of the book: we look in greater detail at classroom implications for the humanities. In this chapter, we look at the significance for the classroom of data-banks, data storage and retrieval; and at the development of the skills that we shall now all need to manage our lives effectively.

We saw, as early as Chapter 1, the extent to which computer operations are already affecting the way we conduct the routines of day to day living. Already, we take for granted the background presence of the electronic information processor and the records it keeps of us. Details of our finances are filed on the bank's computer and brought up to date with every transaction. All this information is quickly available to bank authorities when they need to make decisions, on our credit worthiness for example. If we get into debt, this fact is on computer record — and the information can often be readily available to other traders from whom we seek fresh credit. The unsolicited appeals for mail order bargains that drop through our letter boxes arrive because our names and addresses are on file. In Newcastle our National Insurance status is computer filed and in Swansea a clerk can recall from the computer information about the car we own and the driving licence we carry. We are on the files of insurance companies and of High Street stores. Some of us may well be on police files. Everywhere the computer has made the storage of data vastly more simple and the recall of information astonishingly rapid. No wonder there is great concern about the use to which so much personal information is put and about our own access to it. We worry, too, about the accuracy of the information about us that so many institutions today can store; the file may be electronic but the filer is human! In Chapter 7, we consider how these issues can be discussed in school. In this chapter, we are concerned with the information explosion that computers have made inevitable and how our children can learn the skills to cope.

For though, as citizens, we may justifiably worry about the volume of data now on computer files and issues of privacy, as workers, large numbers of us are even more directly involved. In offices, in shops, in warehouses, in factories data are now kept on computers. Wages, customer information, stock control information — whatever information needs to be readily assessed — is now likely to be on computer. No wonder, as we have seen, there are so many jobs advertised that demand the skills of handling computer filing systems. It is becoming commonplace for worker and manager alike to call up information in a wholly routine manner from some convenient computer terminal.

There is yet more to it than that. If business and government information can be, and is, computerized, then so can virtually any kind of information. Increasingly, we are actually, or potentially, at the receiving end of information on a scale far beyond that possible even with print, radio and television. As a BBC film vividly showed, without computer storage, scientific literature in print would become wholly unmanageable. Research in chemistry, for example, is now computer indexed. Provided a scientist is clear about what he or she wants to know, a computer terminal will rapidly present details of relevant publications or articles saving hours of laborious search through printed abstracts. Increasingly such services are available to the world of learning and could well be extended to schools, as we suggest in Chapter 9. Indeed, there is no reason why there should not be computer access to complete texts — we have already commented on the need to develop screen reading skills and more is said in the following chapter.

If information can be so readily available by computer terminal to the world of learning, it can equally be accessible to every home in the land. In fact, a great deal of information is already at our command via our own TV sets or through a combination of TV, telephone and, more recently, the personal computer. A television set, adapted for teletext, makes available, entirely free, information provided by the BBC and commercial television. Users can call up a range of information — current news, the weather, railway timetables, what's on at cinemas and theatres, shopping information, and so on. Even more significant for all our futures is British Telecom's system of information provision – PRESTEL. Through the telephone line and a suitable adaptor, the home TV set and user are linked to a rapidly-growing information bank supplied by an equally rapidly-growing range of information providers. Already there are nearly 300,000 pages of information at the command of the subscriber. The Council for Educational Technology provides more than 200 pages of continually updated information about education and education resources for schools.

When so much information is at our disposal — and the volume seems likely to grow exponentially over the coming years — then it becomes increasingly important that we know how to handle these systems. How else can we keep any kind of control over our own lives and fashion the community that enables our full human development? To be cut off from the electronic sources of information will, indeed, render us powerless.

We need, then, to know how to understand what it is we want to know. We must learn the skills of questionining as well as those of making effective use of the information we retrieve from the data-banks. The rest of this chapter considers the ways in which information is stored in a computer and how we can retrieve what we need and, thus, the skills that it is becoming increasingly urgent that we teach our children.

Organizing a Data-Bank

The basic organizational principle of a data-bank is not exactly new. We notice that the dust jacket of the current edition of Roget's *Thesaurus* succinctly states the key advantage of the book's system: 'The vocabulary is arranged in numbered groups, each representing an idea, or set of ideas. Cross-references direct the reader to related groups, so opening up a network of associated meanings.' Precisely. As Roget himself remarked in his introduction to his first edition in 1852:

> The purpose of an ordinary dictionary is simply to explain the meaning of the words; and the problem of which it professes to find the solution may be stated thus: – The word being given, to find its signification, or the idea it is intended to convey. The object aimed at in the present undertaking is exactly the converse of this: namely, – The idea being given, to find the word, or words, by which that idea may be most fitly and aptly expressed. For this purpose, the words and phrases of the language are here classed, not according to their sound or their orthography, but strictly according to their *signification*.

The *Thesaurus* principle so described by Roget in 1852, and so brilliantly and thoroughly exemplified in his book, is the principle upon which computer data-banks are organized. They, too, lead us from general ideas to specific facts. Children who, in their English lessons, become familiar with the use of a thesaurus are well on their way to coping with the seeming complexities of PRESTEL. Roget's point is indeed well taken. Experimental work on machine translation of texts (needed simply because of the volume of papers produced and required throughout the world) was bogged down until someone realized that the computer needed programming not with a dictionary but with a thesaurus!

The principle then, for storing information in a data-bank is one of classifications and sub-classifications, sets and sub-sets. So the searcher for information moves from the general to the particular.

Here is a simple example. Suppose you are trying to identify a leaf from a very unfamiliar tree that you have spotted on a walk. Of course, there are books on the market to help but experience does suggest that they are far from easy to use. Suppose now that you have access to data on plant life through such a system as PRESTEL. How do you start? A possibility is that you are asked initially to indicate whether the information you want concerns something animal, vegetable or mineral. Press a key to indicate vegetable; the next *screen* will, perhaps, invite you to choose among a number of plant groups (e.g. trees, shrubs, flowers). Choose trees and you may well find a screen that will ask your choice of a number of aspects of trees (identification, how to grow, timber, geography, etc.). To choose *identification* will lead to another list of choices, usually called a MENU, offering the basic distinction between coniferous and deciduous (perhaps with the old Army distinction of bushy-topped and conical!). This choice made, a further MENU asks for choice of SHAPE, LEAF, BLOSSOM, FRUIT, BARK. Select LEAF and the computer will now show a succession of leaves of, say, deciduous trees. From this, it should be possible to identify the leaf found on the walk. To describe this procedure of selection from successive MENUS takes longer than the search itself. Additionally, there are possibilities of short-circuiting the procedure (for example, if one knows that the leaf is off a deciduous tree).

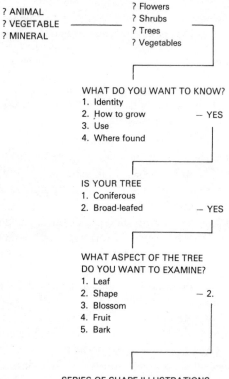

SERIES OF SHAPE ILLUSTRATIONS

What we have just described is the procedure that a user follows — working through a MENU to find the specific piece of information required. As you can see, the procedure does demand a clear sense of what one wants to know.

Consider now how such a program is devised in the first place. To enter information on a computer file, one must think in terms of the information a user might need to extract. Take, for example, a simple home use. We now keep straightforward records of our Open University students on computer file. The lay-out on the screen is just like a card in a conventional card index.

NAME *Jane Smith*	NUMBER *M907 4621 X*
ADDRESS *37 The Bank* *Peole* *High Wycombe HP11 3kz*	TELEPHONE *26218*
PRESENT COURSE *E263*	PREVIOUS COURSES *D101 – 4* *E201 – 2*
TYPE OF SCHOOL *J*	
TUTORIALS *1 – Yes* *2 – No* *3 – No* *4 – Yes*	ASSIGNMENTS *1 – B* *2 – C* *3 – C* *4 – B*
FINAL RESULT *3*	

Each student entry tells us the name of the student, address, official number, course(s) being taken, tutorials attended, assignments submitted with grade, final result, and so on. Information for following years can be entered on the record. What the computer will now do is very rapidly to sort out and display or print precise information as required — for example, all students teaching in junior schools, or all students in a particular location or all students not submitting a particular assignment. The major value of the computer file is just this ability to sort out information that has been requested more rapidly and efficiently than any manual search through a box of cards. The skills we need are:

1. Laying out all the record headings we need
2. Typing in all the individual student details
3. Deciding precisely what information we want that is available to us on the files we have created
4. Telling the computer through a simple command to display that information.

This is the operation that is carried out daily in businesses all over the country. However complex the stored information, retrieving what we want to know is simple enough if (1) the records are satisfactorily designed in the first place, and (2) the computer is asked the right questions.

The example we have just given is that of a simple administrative chore made simpler and more efficient by means of a computer program. In a school, of course, pupil records, staff records, timetabling can all be simplified in such a way. However, what we are concerned with here is helping our pupils to organize information and to make effective use themselves of data-banks to answer their own questions.

Information Skills in the Classroom

What the computer, then, makes possible is the storing and organization in a very compact form of very large stores of information. It also provides a rapid method of retrieving information provided that we know how to define what it is we want to retrieve from the computer store. There are, then, no major new principles involved. We have been using data-banks and filing systems for centuries; they are called *libraries*!

However, we have rather neglected the business of teaching people how to make the best use of these stores. Children are usually given some library lessons. There is some introduction to the organization of a school library and explanation of the commonly used but now largely outdated Dewey system of classification. Children are usually shown how catalogues are arranged in accordance with Dewey. Some work is done on the use of reference books such as encyclopaedias. The Bullock Report in 1974 noted the importance of dealing efficiently with information:

> It becomes increasingly necessary for a person not only to be able to cope with print efficiently, but to organise his own use of it. This means that he must be able to identify his own information needs, a much less simple matter than it sounds ... Pupils should be led to confidence in the use of bibliographical tools and in tapping sources of information in the community at large, and as the sources of information continue to change and multiply the teacher must be prepared to learn alongside his pupil.[1]

Bullock commented thus in the light of the Committee's survey which showed, *inter alia*, that there were still 26% of schools where libraries were used partly as classrooms and where 70% of secondary schools had fewer than the number of books per pupil (10) in their libraries recommended by the Library Association. In 1981, six years after the Bullock Report, the Schools Council publication, *Information Skills in the Secondary Curriculum*[2], continues to emphasize the point:

> Never before has so much information been available to so many, and never

before have our lives depended so much on our ability to handle information successfully. We need to be able to search out what we require, to assess critically the ideas and facts offered to us, and to make use of our findings. . .And yet the schools, which are concerned with learning above all else, find great difficulty in teaching pupils *how* to learn. . . .It is a central responsibility of the school to help its pupils cope with learning. [3]

The Bullock survey also noted, what unfortunately remains a commonplace observation in many schools — the time spent on copying and reproducing material from books. It is not just a matter of the usually pointless copying of chunks from library books that can be seen in some topic or project work but the burden of unproductive note making and blackboard copying that still goes on up to and even in the sixth form. This was a point also emphasized by HMI in *Aspects of Secondary Education*. [4] The authors recently asked their own group of PGCE students (would-be English specialists from many parts of the country) about their own experience of information skills in school and university. They had little to report save a sense that all would have welcomed more positive teaching, more practical help in becoming autonomous learners.

There is much to be done with print; the arrival of the computer in no way removes from schools the responsibility of teaching pupils how to handle books and printed documents, how to read effectively for purposes defined by readers themselves. What the computer can do is to facilitate this teaching of information skills and help both pupils and teachers out of the rut we have been briefly describing. Use of a computer data-bank compels the use of an effective questioning technique.

Some schools are already working with computerized data. We mentioned one such school in Chapter 1 and its use of census returns. There will be further examples in this section of the book as we discuss the classroom use of the micro in the various subjects of the humanities curriculum. In some parts of the country, schools have been linked to data-banks run by local authorities or colleges on a time-sharing basis. There are some school experiments in the classroom use of PRESTEL — though this can prove very expensive in terms of telephone costs; there is an urgent need for materials that will enable schools to teach teletext skills without incurring such costs so that pupils will only use PRESTEL itself when they know enough to ensure economy in use. All these are useful activities that will undoubtedly grow and develop very fast in the years ahead. One of the most valuable features, for example, of the BBC micro is that it can be linked to PRESTEL and similar systems to give schools access not only to information pages but also to computer program facilities in the network which can then be downloaded into the microcomputer. The major educational and commercial potential of the PRESTEL system lies in its capacity to be interactive.

However, these are all data-banks held outside the school. They are, in the main, resources designed for purposes other than teaching. If pupils are to acquire the skills they will need for access to and control over information sources, then they will need to learn:

1. How to create their own files; and
2. How to use their files to answer their own questions.

The report of the Bryanston Seminar (held in Cambridge in October 1981) had this to say:

> A starting point may well be a 'Twenty Questions' type game based on the children in the room, allowing Yes/No answers about them, which draws attention to the way in which information can be classified in sets. The computer would then be used with an introductory program illustrating the uses to which this technique can be put. . .

> In creating a data base, children would be expected to:

> (a) decide on the subject
> (b) brainstorm to select particular features
> (c) establish the scale of the exercise and the type of information to be fed into the computer
> (d) collect a sample of the information and pilot its use
> (e) modify and complete the collection
> (f) test the data base

> In using the program:

> (a) children must be able to show how information can be retrieved
> (b) children must be taught to isolate, evaluate and use the information [5]

A major consequence of the Bryanston Seminar on *Micro-electronics and the Humanities* has, in fact, been the publication by Cambridge University Press in conjunction with the Microelectronics Education Programme, of a program (with full teaching notes) doing precisely what is described above. This is FACTFILE designed by Daniel Chandler. FACTFILE contains two programs. The first is introductory — to show children how a computer file works. Children supply the computer with information about themselves under a number of headings in answer to questions on the screen. They can then retrieve this information about themselves sorted in all sorts of different ways. The second program enables children to make their own files on a subject of their own choice. They have to decide their own 'headings' — that is the kinds of information they are going to enter into their files. For example (as has been done a number of times by children) a group may decide to create a data bank on Dinosaurs. The children will have undertaken the following steps to create the bank:

1. List the dinosaurs to be included:
2. Sort them into groups (size? kind of food? means of locomotion?);
3. Settle on the categories of information to be input for each dinosaur.

Of course, the information to be input must come from somewhere. The children are now involved in library work. They need to get hold of reference books on dinosaurs; there are plenty around! They now need to use the books to list the various extinct reptiles and to extract, for each, the information they have decided they want to bank (size, weight, locomotion, diet, life span, etc.). This is a *group* responsibility, just as it was when they decided on the headings.

The sets of information are fed into a computer that has been prepared by the children to accept information under the headings they want. The children can now retrieve information in the form that they want it, for the computer can rapidly sort it for them. What carnivorous reptiles could fly? Is there a link between size and diet (vegetarians over 10 metres long, say, and meat eaters less than 10 metres long)?

FACTFILE is very flexible and can be used by children to create useful data banks on any topic of their choice. It has been designed for young children (7 – 9-year-olds) and there is no doubt at all about the enthusiastic and efficient use the children make of the program.

FACTFILE is comparatively simple. After all, it has been written for young children. But the potential is enormous if one thinks about larger and more complex files of information. A great strength of this kind of program is the control exercised by the users. They settle on the subject; they decide what information is to be filed. As a consequence, they have a retrieval system geared to their own needs and interests. Consider, too, the educational value of designing such a file and coming to a consensus in the group about what is to be stored, as well as the ease with which such computer files can be added to, amended or even changed.

Precisely the same approach can be used to teach older pupils. All the micros in school use have programs enabling the filing of information under appropriate heads. One of the authors has a cheap, commercially-produced cassette for the Sinclair Spectrum which not only provides such a program but also offers an example — a gazetteer of countries of the world with, for each country, its capital city, languages spoken, currency, gross national product, etc. As the notes say: 'This file can be interrogated and manipulated with all the commands of VU*FILE' — that is, the instructions that the program has been written to accept.

In this kind of work, then, children are learning how to sort out information to meet their own needs. At the same time, they are learning how to use printed sources of information in an organized way; they are learning the valuable skills of skimming and scanning. This kind of work is a far remove from pointless copying. The evidence, so far, shows that children over a wide range of ability gain from this work of this kind with a computer. Discussion is involved in settling on categories of information and, later, in deciding on the questions necessary for retrieval. To this all contribute. As a bonus, poorer readers seem to gain from the experience of using the computer keyboard.

Here is another example devised by a Norfolk school and reported in *Computer Software for Schools*.[6] It provides a program for, in effect, cataloguing the library and other school information resources. The authors note the problem children have in finding information that does actually provide the details they need in a form with which they can cope. A simple program would enable authors and titles to be sorted by themes (e.g., horses, fishing, football, etc.). A more complex program, developed by the school, allows resources to be coded in the computer under feature (topic, part of the world, period of history) and also under format (book, booklet, computer program, magazine, map, slide set, tape). All this is in addition to a basic subject classification. A user can identify what he or she wants, then, in terms of subject, topic within the subject and format. Location among the school resources is thus greatly simplified and useful study time saved. Typically, the information is retrieved by a series of menus. At first, the choice is of main subject. Then the user must choose the appropriate topic code or codes (e.g., items on pollution in Germany). The computer response will be a list of resources with their format and location in the school. An earlier attempt to do this was the OCCI Index — this was a punched card system. It worked — if one was manually dextrous enough! It was also very large and cumbersome and time-consuming. Ten years ago it seemed the latest thing in information retrieval. Now it is virtually obsolete.

There are today a number of other developments in language work in schools that are helpful. The Open University Diploma in Reading Development firmly put information skills on the INSET agenda for teachers. Students of these courses are clearly having a marked influence on practice. There are teacher groups now in various parts of the country devising materials to assist in the development of study skills. There are books on the market (more each year) including the authors' own series *English Skills*.[7] The Schools Council Project *The Effective Use of Reading*,[8] under the direction of Eric Lunzer and Keith Gardner, has moved beyond careful identification of needs and beyond the delineation of a sound theoretical base into the devising of practical materials for teachers and classrooms. When DARTS (Directed Activities Relating to Texts) become generally available in the forthcoming publication *Learning from the Written Word*,[9] they will undoubtedly combine usefully with anything a school is doing to teach the skills discussed in this chapter. The chapter on work in English and related language arts that follows will say more about reading skills among other matters. At this point, it is enough to stress the crucial link between the development of what are sometimes called Higher Order skills in reading (including comprehension) and the skills needed to read the VDU in the process of creating a data-bank or retrieving information from it.

We conclude this chapter by summarizing a program from the United States which, it seems to us, exemplifies the educational qualities we have been advocating. The program is fully described in *The Use and Misuse of Computers in Education* by Allan B. Ellis. [10] As this book is not easily obtainable in Britain, we make no apologies for detailed references to it. It seems to us a very important book in the clarity of its thinking and its excellent sense. Alan Ellis has confirmed, strengthened and greatly extended our own thinking about the potential of computers in education. The use of the computer he describes arose out of a project designed to help schools in Massachussetts cope more effectively with the problems of vocational guidance — careers advice is not always as useful as it might be in schools either in the United States or in Britain. What careers advice does at its best is to help a young man or woman towards personal decision making based on a clearer understanding both of self and of opportunities. Arriving at such a decision is a very complex process involving a great deal of thinking and feeling as well as depending upon the availability of information at the right times.

Ellis suggests that there are two main stages in the process. First, there is a process of *anticipation*. We are preoccupied with the 'pieces' — facts, alternatives, options, consequences — that go to make a decision. We are also involved in the hopes and doubts that go to determine a decision. In the next stage we move from anticipation to *accommodation* when we begin to match imagination against reality.

Throughout the whole of this decision-taking process, a young man or woman looking into a career must continually process data. As the data come from the real world, they will never be complete and that is why choices are necessary. The information does not contain the decisions; the student must make those his, or her, own responsibility.

However, in order to make choices a student must be placed among resources. The problem that the project directors then faced was that of easy access to resources — a problem indeed as anyone who has faced the mass of career literature will appreciate. The project team quickly saw the advantages of occupational data being readily available on a computer.

> But placing the student among resources is just part of what the guidance theory requires. It requires, as well, that the student gets help as he engages in the decision-making process . . . First, he must have the opportunity to browse through a large set of resources within the system and to obtain cues from the system as he goes. Browsing is an unstructured activity, but it is not an aimless one; and, therefore, the system should facilitate the emergence of order by probing, suggesting, reminding and generally being at the individual's disposal. Second, the student needs the ability to follow up leads, discard them, go as far as he wishes and then start anew. There should be available to him projections and estimates about himself with which he may compare his own interests and abilities to those of others who have taken certain courses of action. . . . Finally, he needs a way to relive his past in terms

of his present orientation and to act out the future or, perhaps, to bring his awareness of the future to bear upon his current need to make a career decision. The system must contain some kind of stimulator or game player, therefore, which can process student data within the larger context of data about the world of work so that the student can engage in what amounts to a "career game".

The following diagram shows the broad pattern of the set of programs the project produced. The introduction gets basic personal information from the student and shows him how the system works. The Major Orientation program elicits from the student his or her broad current area of interest so that he or she can go to an appropriate orientation set of programs. The system allows browsing among the programs before a student moves towards any firm decision. A simulation career game is also available to help in this process.

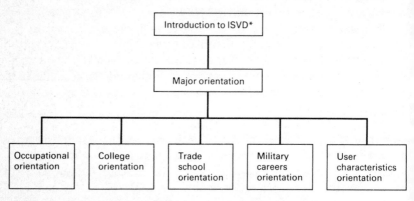

* Information System for Vocational Decisions

Each of the four occupational sets of programs are, in effect, data bases. The occupational data base, for instance, contains facts on some 850 occupations. The user characteristics data-base gradually collects information about the student moving through the system, monitoring his activities. The following extract, quoted by Ellis, gives some idea as to how the program proceeds:

> Our student (called Cohen) is not too sure whether he wants to go to college and certainly does not know enough about what is entailed. The Major Orientation program sends Cohen along to a further orientation program that is part of the collection of programs dealing with colleges. This is what happens:
>
> *Computer:*   The activities you can request are: Select a School, Data about certain schools, Exploring your interests, Factors colleges use in admission, Tests, Size of School, College Life, Transfer, or Scholarships.

Try to be specific but use simple words. What would you like to do now?

Cohen: It is difficult to say. What can I do?

Computer: 1. Choose a College
2. Direct data access
3. Explore Colleges
4. Tests
5. Cooperative programs
6. Cost of College
7. Living arrangements
8. Paying for College
9. Size of Schools

Cohen: I still do not know which thing I want to do.

Computer: A list of the more interesting things to do in the ISVD* follows. Each suggestion will be followed by a chance for you to type YES and try that or NO and get another suggestion.

Would you like to select a College by listing your preference?

Cohen: I am not ready for that yet.

Computer: Would you like to ask for facts about a specific School?

Cohen: That is much too specific.

Computer: Are you interested in factors Colleges use in selecting the Freshman Class?

Cohen: Yes. That is exactly what I need.

So Cohen is now transferred by the computer to just such a program. Note that the computer is not bothered by Cohen taking little notice of the instructions! It will continue to list alternatives until Cohen types the one word YES.

The computer program then provides facts about the college admission procedures and how they select applicants. Later, Cohen can use the system to get details of particular colleges and the courses they offer.

This is a complex set of programs and not wholly easy for the user to handle. Nevertheless it is a lot easier than ploughing through a library of vocational material and any interview, face to face, with a careers adviser is made more useful simply because so much of the vital groundwork has already been done by the student. A student will make mistakes on such a set of programs — although the programs themselves are arranged so as to offer help in case of difficulty. But a student learns how to ask questions and, in so doing, learns about himself or herself. More important, the student feels that he or she is in control of the system and making the decisions. The speed of the computer in sorting through large banks of data to find the information that is requested reduces frustration considerably and that, too, helps reflection. It is important, though, to stress that students are not abandoned to the computer. There remains the need for the human counsellor with whom to discuss provisional decisions and their implications.

This has been a brief summary of a complex set of computer programs. Ellis gives a full description. Enough has been said, we hope, to indicate some of the crucial features of what we believe to be valuable uses of the computer as an information processor. The system allows for user input. It is large enough to encourage purposeful browsing. It is logically constructed so that a user can find a way to what is needed. It encourages a user, or group of users, to make informed decisions.

The computer, then, is a powerful aid to teaching, a powerful aid to helping our students to become autonomous learners. We shall see other developments of the machine's educational potential in following chapters — all encouraging the skills of questioning, of exploration.

6

The 'Language Arts' Curriculum

We have preferred to use the terminology customary in North America of 'the Language Arts' rather than English for the educationally central processes of learning to use language in all its modes (talking, listening, reading, writing) in order to try to cut through many of the basic assumptions and prejudices that arise when many, especially secondary, teachers think about the English curriculum. In *New Directions in English Teaching* Adams[1] comments upon how slow schools have been to adjust to the processes of technological change so that the serious study of even television as the primary medium of communication and cultural transmission is still regarded as unusual in the English curriculum in British schools in the 1980s. Unless we can both adapt and update the English curriculum there is a real danger that, by the year 2000, English teaching in our schools will be in the same position of decline as classical studies today. The world will have passed it by and what we have traditionally thought of as English studies, the subject of the battles of the sixties that we are still fighting, will become the preserve of an eccentric few. The term 'Language Arts' with its emphasis upon language and upon communication studies seems to us to be a helpful one and it also succeeds in stressing the 'across the curriculum' element of such studies. The place to develop and practise one's skills in this area of the curriculum is certainly not the English classroom alone. Primary teachers, on the other hand, have generally seen themselves as teachers of language in the first instance though this is not to devalue the important place that the experience of literature, as seen in 'story', has always played in their work. One reason why the National Association for the Teaching of English (NATE) has failed, over twenty years now, to attract infant and primary teachers to join its membership must lie in its name. If it were being formed today it would, perhaps, be more appropriate to call it something like the National Association for Education in and through Language. It is, therefore, upon the language element in the curriculum that this chapter will focus, whatever timetabled place this may find in the school.

The reference to the four language modes in the last paragraph deliberately placed the skills of *oracy* (talking, listening) before those of *literacy* (reading, writing) yet we know from much in the way of research and surveys, including the HMI study *Aspects of Secondary Education*[2] (see Chapter 4) how little time is actually given to the processes of talk in the classroom. Yet all the evidence from the working world, as explored in Chapter 4, makes it clear that oracy skills are of paramount importance in the world outside school. In considering some of the ways in which we need to adapt we saw the increased development of skills of oral communication and increased confidence in oneself as a communicator as being educationally of the first importance. Here is one area where the introduction of the microcomputer into the classroom can be of very great help to the teacher.

We dealt earlier with some of the managerial problems that will be met on first introducing the microcomputer into the classroom. However, one major reason for the neglect of talk in the classroom is also the managerial problems involved. Teachers still do not know enough about how to handle talk, how to ensure that the students are and remain motivated to talk about the topic that has been proposed to them and how to monitor the effects of the talking that takes place. In all of these areas the microcomputer can be of considerable help. Coping with the management problems it presents will paradoxically help to overcome some of those presented by talk in the classroom. If we see the most likely use of the microcomputer as being with groups of students working at a single terminal, then what they are doing at the terminal provides an immediate focus for the talk that is to go on within the group. If, for example, they are engaged in some problem-solving activity (as they will frequently be even if the problem is only to formulate an appropriate question with which to interrogate the available data) the group has to talk its way through the problem and, since only one solution can be input into the terminal, the group has through discussion to reach a consensus as to which answer they find acceptable. In Adams and Pearce[3] it was suggested that one reason why students were not very good at using talk to solve problems ('transactional talk' as it were) was because we did not give them sufficient opportunity to practise this kind of talking. We do not, in fact, place a very high value generally in education upon pupils' ability to find out and to make knowledge for themselves through talking. Yet the work of Barnes[4] and others has demonstrated conclusively how important to the whole learning process this kind of 'problem-solving' talk ought to be, and Weber in *The Teacher is the Key*[5] has shown very convincingly how children with learning difficulties can be given enhanced confidence and develop the skills necessary for learning once they are given problems to solve, irrespective of the content of the problems themselves. So Weber uses highly motivating puzzles of the brain teaser kind in order to develop such skills as those involved in following and articulating sequential trains of thought. It is easy to see how material of this kind lends itself to being put on a computer program; indeed, many of the games commercially produced for home entertainment depend upon logical

processes of this kind; see the very successful series of *Adventure* type games
for example. The point to be stressed is that, even at the lowest level and
working with what might in other respects be a very limited program indeed,
groups of students who are trying to solve the problem presented to them and
to agree upon their answer and are then testing it by seeing the consequences
of inputting it to the terminal, are learning something in the process itself.
Chandler has pointed out how Adventure games, very closely linked as a genre
to the role-play games 'Dungeons and Dragons', can be used 'to encourage
positive role-play, lateral thinking and democratic decision-making [so as to] —
form a motivating centrepiece for a variety of group language activities.' He
describes how, in playing 'Mission Impossible', a game in a modern setting
where the object is to prevent a nuclear reactor from exploding by finding and
defusing a saboteur's time bomb, the group interaction becomes of crucial
importance:

> The game proceeds, through rooms and corridors, with students having to
> decide how to open locked doors, evade security cameras and ultimately
> defuse the bomb. As one student commented, 'the advantage of playing the
> game in a group is that you can all put your ideas forward of what to do next.'
> . . . Another student added the profound comment that working in a group
> makes the game more than just 'a private struggle against the machine'.[6]

In this particular version of the Adventure game the computer will only accept
instructions in sentences composed of two words and it operates with only a
very limited vocabulary. If it is asked to respond to anything which it considers too difficult an apologetic message appears on the screen:

"I don't know how to . . . something", or
"I don't know what . . . is".

Chandler's comment on this seeming limitation is very interesting:

> Some teachers might regard it as a limitation that students are able to use
> sentences of only two words in length, with its consequent contortions of
> conventional grammar. On the contrary, I have found the computer's
> responses to words it does not understand . . . have been very useful indeed
> as a dynamic demonstration of the concept of verb and subject. Students tend
> to treat their group as an instant thesaurus when the computer insists, 'I must
> be stupid but I don't understand what you mean'.

Our own experience of playing this game confirms Chandler's view. It is, at
first, frustrating to have to find ways of rephrasing what one wants done in
terms that the computer will 'understand' and so accept. But the doing of this
calls for all manner of linguistic resources and working in a pair or a group
maximizes the inventive and linguistic powers that can be brought to bear
upon the developing problem. Moreover to 'solve' the problems presented by

the game, the players have by a process of trial and error, and memory, to work their way into the mind of the compiler, to reconstruct in their minds, or in the form of a drawing on paper perhaps, the tangle of tunnels and communicating doors that make up the maze within which the game is set. This, in its turn, calls for other linguistic skills, and for the linking of skills of talking and deducing with those of graphicacy. Furthermore with a little extra effort and ingenuity other language activities can be built around the game — extra clues can be provided in coded form, for example, or there can be a further trail of instructions that can only be followed if the right information is obtained from conventional print sources in a library. It is quite possible to operate this game with thirty students working in four or five groups with each group taking its turn at the terminal and carrying on where the previous group left off while the other groups are occupied with different, but related, language activities, thus solving at one go the managerial problems introduced by both talk and the micro in the classroom. (For those schools which possses a BBC Computer Model B the game 'Philosopher's Quest' is a particularly entertaining and demanding example of the genre.)

We would not, of course, wish to seem to be making too much in the way of claims for games of this kind. Their main use is to provide an entertaining opportunity for group discussion and, through the computer program, to provide a self-monitoring capacity whereby the results of the discussion can be tried out. An added advantage is that having made a decision and communicated that decision to the machine you have to go on playing while living with the consequence of the decision you have just made, be it, in the end, a wise or foolish one. The game itself is only a means to an end, the primary educational focus is the talk, although there may be other incidental lessons being learned such as the value of co-operation and ways of working together amicably as a group. An analogy is to be found in a card game developed as part of a programme in Peace Studies described by a Mr Peter Davies as a splendid example of the subject in action:

> A group of six children were each given an envelope containing variously shaped pieces of card and told to form them into a square — an impossible task unless they helped one another.

> It takes about 15 minutes to twig you have actually got to give people part of your own resources in order to achieve what you need . . . An awful lot of children don't think about cooperation and there is a lot less cooperation within the classroom than there should be. There is far less discussion among children than they need to have to understand each other.[7]

But games of this kind need to be sharply differentiated in our thinking from the simulation type game that is more familiar in many of our humanities and social studies classrooms. These we deal with in a later chapter. The point we would want to make here is that games *which do not in themselves teach anything* can be of use in the language arts classroom by reason of the language practice they may make possible.

One added advantage of using the microcomputer for playing games of this kind is that it leaves the students to play the game uninterrupted (and therefore unhelped) by the teacher. They can be left alone as a group with the computer. Our experience of playing similar games without a computer both with teachers and student teachers in the classroom (see, for example, Weber's excellent game 'The Crowfoot Expedition', reprinted in Adams, Butterworth and Jones, *English Skills 3*[8]) is that it is very difficult to resist the temptation to interfere, to get in the way and to make sure that the pupils are going 'along the right lines'; one positive value that the introduction of the micro brings is that it gets the teacher out of the way and so allows the pupils to make the mistakes, and the discoveries, for themselves. This also frees the teacher, of course, to interact directly with one or more of the other groups engaged in related work along the lines already suggested.

A major limitation of all the commercially produced Adventure type games that we have been describing is that in the end, however tortuously conceived by the compiler, they do have some kind of a linear structure. There is, finally, only one right answer which it is the object of the game to uncover. But we are likely to see more intelligently conceived games of the type developed specifically for educational purposes in the near future. Chandler is currently working on a computer game, provisionally called 'Magic, Force and Reason', which is a combination of an Adventure game and a story generator. When completed, it will enable children of middle, or lower secondary, age to develop a story which is also a game. The players will be able to define the environment in which the game is set, invent characters endowed with particular qualities who will then interact with each other, but whose behaviour will have to be consistent within the framework already established. The goals of the game will be defined by the players but the characters will need to ensure that 'they have enough warmth, food, water, rest and general "good health" to survive'. They will only be able to do this through cooperation as a group since the survival of one 'character' will depend also upon the survival of the group as a whole and each character will have certain unique powers on which the group as a whole depends. Chandler sees a clear link here with the fairly conventional 'English' activity of group story-telling:

> The tasks of the game author . . . are essentially those of the story-teller. She must devise a 'plot' which will hold her audience even more than in a conventional context. Games must, first and foremost, be entertaining. She has no choice but to avoid making this simply sequential: her 'readers' have too much freedom of choice. The story's direction is under the control of the participants, so they too are telling a story . . . Inadequacies in planning actually matter far more than in a printed story: if the author doesn't rewrite it, the players will.[9]

In its present form Chandler's 'game' is clearly much influenced by 'Dungeons and Dragons' with its fantasy format and with the 'game author' here taking over the role of the 'dungeon master'. But, once the idea is established, it is easy to see how other kinds of conventional plot-formats might be adapted along similar lines, the desert island or the kidnapped story for example. In this way the computer as a focus for group story composition (or 'story-boarding') could be seen as a way of leading into and out of the exploration of conventional fantasy and adventure literature. We are not far away from the possibility of having Leon Garfield's world of eighteenth century London (itself a fantasy creation) as the basis for a computer game which will both motivate and enhance the reading of his novels, for example.

Even while this chapter was being written an advertisement appeared for what could be the first in a new generation of 'Adventure' type games. This is a game based upon the plot and characters of J.R.R. Tolkien's *The Hobbit*, a copy of which is provided when you purchase the program. The claims made are large ones:

> In this program you take on the role of Bilbo, the hobbit: danger, adventure and excitement are all part of it, presented to you in words and graphics, but it is you who must confront and solve the problems this time.
>
> You instruct the computer in completely ordinary English sentences! . . .
>
> You will meet all your favourite characters from J.R.R. Tolkien's book, and amazing as it sounds, they will all have an independent life of their own. They can make decisions and act on them! They react not only to what you do, but also to every other character in *The Hobbit*!
>
> Because of this unique feature, you will find that each time you play *The Hobbit*, events will proceed in a slightly different way, and *the further you get into Tolkien's world*, the more different each visit may be . . .
>
> *The Hobbit* program follows closely the plot of the book . . . (our italics)[10]

The reviews indicate that it is not quite so revolutionary in conception as the advertisement suggests. Nonetheless, it is the first attempt we have come across to base this kind of game on an actual work of literature and the review in *Your Computer* (January 1983) does make it clear that 'it helps to have read the book in finding your way around'. Our own experience of playing confirms this and certainly the game provokes a great deal of animated discussion. There seems no reason why this kind of game should not be further developed, and every likelihood that it will be, probably with better and more complex novels than *The Hobbit* as a base.

All this may seem, and doubtless is, a long way from the conventional teaching of 'literature' in schools. But it would be absurd not to suppose that the new technology will develop new artistic potential of its own. With the launch of the BBC Computer the WELCOME package that was produced to give users a taste of the potential of the machine included a poem by Roger McGough that exploited some of these possibilities. The user (reader?) was invited to cooperate with the poet in suggesting names and situations and the graphics capacity of the machine was used so that the words moved about and enacted their meaning on the screen. At present this kind of development is in a very primitive form and one does not suppose that even its author would make very good literary claims for this particular 'poem'. It may, however, be the first example of a kind of kinetic poetry, an enhanced development out of concrete poetry where we shall literally see words in action on the screen. If so, and if we exploit in literary terms the capability for interaction between the microcomputer and the 'reader', we are likely to see some very interesting new developments in literature before long. One of us was recently at a conference on English teaching in Canada where large claims were being made for the possibilities of the literature of the future being created in this way providing infinite possibilities for the development of the story by the reader. The recent Cambridge University Press series of books for schools, *Story-Trails*,[11] is an interesting example of the same kind of thing being done in conventional publishing terms with a series of alternative possible developments from amongst which the reader is invited to choose. We are already familiar, in other contexts, with 'take part' books and books where the story is personalized around a particular reader — you are invited to send in the name of your child who becomes the hero of the story — all this can be done on a wider and more complex scale by using the potential of the microcomputer. It could be that in developing story-telling skills, including purely conventional literary skills like the handling of narrative, we are preparing students in school to cope with the likely development of new literary forms in the age of the microcomputer. We would not wish the seeming flights of fancy in the above paragraphs to be misunderstood, however. There does not seem any likelihood of conventional literature being made obsolete by the microcomputer any more than Shakespeare was made obsolete by the invention of television. But the coming of television made possible new literary forms (television drama) and new ways of interpreting the old (Shakespeare on television); it would be naive not to expect the latest developments in technology and the microchip to have their aesthetic and cultural spin-off as well. Indeed it would be tragically arid were they not to do so!

Certainly so far as the adaptation of the microcomputer to this element of the Language Arts curriculum is concerned we are hardly dealing in the realms of the future at all. Sharples[12] has described in some detail an experiment based at the University of Edinburgh where there was a pilot project seeking to develop a course in computer-based creative writing for 11 – 12 year-olds. What is interesting about his account is the very carefully structured nature of the language teaching that had to be devised in order that they might get the best out of the potential of the computer available to them.

The course accordingly split into two sections in the first of which the children developed their understanding and manipulation of language. This gave them a foundation for the second part of the course in which they explored and improved their written style. (It is no accident that Sharples is clearly much influenced by structural linguistics and that his program is one of the first of which we are aware to try to link together, through the potential of the microcomputer, the serious training of linguistic skills with the creativity of story-telling. It provides precisely the discipline that was so often lacking in earlier, now largely discredited, approaches to creative writing. Further development of work along these lines may lead to a much greater sense of craft on the part of the student-writer and a much greater need for linguistic understanding on the part of the teacher.) The whole of Sharples' account is worth reading but the following extract will give the flavour of the very interesting teaching involved:

> The children were . . . introduced to the constraints and conventions of story content, again through games and exercises. In one game a group of children wrote a description of an unusual picture; the decription was passed to another group who attempted to redraw the picture, guided only by the written description. This proved to be a useful exercise of descriptive completeness — one group's description, for instance, omitted any mention of colour; the second team complained that they could not draw the picture as they had no idea which coloured crayons to use. From the exercises the children formed a strategy and checklist for descriptive composition. They were then encouraged to break down the process of descriptive writing into manageable stages — planning, draft writing, revision — with the aid of a computer based game. The children were split into two groups. Each group drew up a plan of the rooms of a haunted house and then wrote descriptions of each room, plus details of treasure and the occupants of the house. The descriptions were incorporated into a game, similar to the popular 'Adventure' game and the opposing group then 'explored' the house, fought off the inhabitants and found the treasure by typing commands to the program.

Working with, admittedly, a very small experimental group of children Sharples found a dramatic improvement in the student's capacity to manipulate language and revise text. With one group of pupils, who showed no great interest in the story-telling part of the experiment and who were therefore not put through the second part of the experimental programme, they instead:

> . . . used a computer text processor to compose, modify and print descriptive pieces. Once they discovered that the computer could aid the tedious process of revision and presentation, their interest in writing increased and they produced articles for a class newsletter and items for the children's page of the local Edinburgh newspaper.

Such work is a good example of the ways in which the use of a microcomputer can be effectively dovetailed with quite traditional approaches to English teaching. Sharples' experiments are not unique. He cites examples of similar work which is already well advanced in the United States where, even at College level, computer programs are being used to 'prompt' writing, to help students by asking them salient questions to encourage more vivid and accurate descriptive writing.

Similarly, Jones describes a program for infant schools where a 'story setting' is provided by a random generation of a display of three characters, a setting and an action, all of which can be set in the past present and future. He points out also that the same program can be used to generate story-board situations which can be used for drama. Most interestingly of all in this context he cites:

> . . . an upper junior/lower secondary version of this program with data supplied by fourth-year junior school children. They have included some very interesting settings (20 of them) and 16 different actions as well as 35 different characters! The unusual juxtaposition of such characters, settings and actions has resulted in some excellent writing, for it offers far more of a stimulus than a single title, and it can be so individualised.[13]

Seen in these terms the microcomputer in the Language Arts classroom can be regarded as a kind of equivalent to the old-fashioned kaleidoscope which provided ideas for the artist to work on by suggesting possibilities; in the same way the computer program can help to get ideas flowing for the student who 'doesn't know what to write about' or who has problems over writing anything copiously.

All this brings us to what is, necessarily for the Language Arts teacher, the primary application of the microcomputer to the classroom — that is its use as a word processor. At the very least the ability to correct the first draft of a text with ease and with the avoidance of the tediousness of having to write the whole thing out again leads to a greater willingness on the part of the student to redraft and proof-read the work. The motivation of seeing it well presented on a screen or printed out as 'hard copy' is a very powerful one and provides a genuine incentive to 'get it right' in the student's own terms. Most teachers of English have spent many hours typing out students' work for display purposes and for publication as class magazines in the belief that a major way of motivating and encouraging reluctant writers is to let them see what their work will look like when it is properly presented. Now, with the computer as a writing instrument, we can hand over that task to the students themselves and they can gain the immediate and personal satisfaction of seeing their work as they would, ideally, like to see it presented. Frank Smith, in his important book *On Writing and the Writer*[14] testifies to the improvement in students' willingness to revise their text when given a word processor to help them to do so and Seymour Papert in *Mindstorms* makes a similar point:

> . . . for most children rewriting a text is so laborious that the first draft is the
> final copy, and the skill of re-reading with a critical eye is never acquired . . .
> this changes dramatically when children have access to computers capable of
> manipulating text . . . I have seen a child move from total rejection of writing
> to an intense involvement (accompanied by rapid improvement of quality)
> within a few weeks of beginning to write with a computer.[15]

A very similar point has been made in an important article by Daniel Watt
in *Popular Computing* describing work with a 12-year old, Tina, with severe
learning difficulties. He demonstrates the improvement in her motivation and
performance as a result of being given access to a word processor:

> For an entire hour, Tina painstakingly typed a two-line letter to her aunt.
> Although her expression was idiosyncratic and her spelling and punctuation
> were irregular, she worked slowly and thoughtfully. When her letter was
> printed out looking perfect and professional, Tina was thrilled. She insisted
> on making several copies, giving them to her teachers and friends as well as
> sending the 'original' to her aunt.[16]

Clearly, even in conventional writing terms, the microcomputer has
potential as 'automatic Tippex'. It can work more effectively than even a conventional electric typewriter in enabling us to correct errors, improve spelling
and punctuation. We can proof-read and edit, and still end up with a
beautifully-produced piece of work without having to go through the labour
of rewriting the whole thing again. It provides the experienced, no less than
the neophyte, writer with the incentive to get the text as perfect as it is possible
for it to be. But, potentially, this is of much less significance than the
realization of the full potential of the computer-as-word-processor as a
machine capable of *manipulating* text. Watt goes so far as to say that the word
processor, by which he means the potential to type, edit, store, print and
communicate the written word, is 'a perfect example of an invention whose
uses couldn't be imagined until it existed'. Now, for the first time without
laborious repetition, we can try out what we want to say in different ways,
move paragraphs around, change and insert sentences, replace and substitute
words and ideas, and still have a perfect copy for our final version. A wholly
new dimension is given to W.H. Auden's famous dictum: 'How do I know
what I mean until I see what I say?' for we can be encouraged, as few writers
have ever been before, to experiment with a whole range of ways of saying the
same thing and this can be done with no more tedium or physical labour than
writing a first draft with a pen, or at a typewriter. Joyce was reputed to have
spent a whole day composing a fifteen-word sentence in *Ulysses*, trying out
every possible combination of the words to give the exact meaning he was
looking for; now the word processor brings the capacity to do this kind of
playing about with what we are writing *while we are writing it* within the

potential of every student in every classroom. It seems undeniable that the microprocessor has brought about conditions that will significantly affect our whole approach to the composing process and that, for students and professional writers of the future, writing and composing will become a much less linear process than hitherto.

Several other considerations are cognate with the above. We take for granted that the student of the near future will be quite familiar with the processes of keyboard skills and screen-reading, neither of them quite as straightforward as they may seem. But these are, as we have seen in Chapter 1, already the literacy skills that are needed as soon as a student leaves school to go into many jobs in industry or commerce. We must seek to develop these psycho-motor skills at a very early age so that they become as much second nature as, for most children, the manipulation of pencil or pen. But for this to be possible there must be an adequate supply of terminals in a school and students must be encouraged to have recourse to them as a primary writing medium. It is significant that the article already mentioned by Watt deals with a student, Tina, with learning difficulties. His conclusion is stark, but, we think, over-pessimistic:

> Will word processing make a difference in the way *some* children learn to write? I'm convinced that it will. The most likely candidates are children who have computers in their homes. These are generally the children of well-educated, affluent parents who understand the advantages of learning to write well. Will word processing make a difference in the way most children learn to write? In the short-term future, it probably will not. Word processing requires expensive equipment: computers with lots of memory, disk drives, and printers. More important, word processing requires lots of hands-on time for every writer. Even a school with a computer in every classroom simply won't be able to provide students with enough access time to make a difference . . . Unless we change our educational priorities by the time word processing starts to get passed around, the Tinas of this world are going to be left out.

However, a start (however limited) can be made with a Sinclair ZX81 computer and printer and, if we see a computer in every classroom as a desirable aim (and one that is surely achievable in the not too distant future), the proper management of what happens in the classroom should allow at least some 'hands-on' time and experience for all our students. After all, most schools have commerce and typing departments equipped with expensive electric typewriters; if we accept the view that traditional typewriting is now obsolescent we can begin to prepare our students to live in the world that will await them when they leave school. It does seem important to us that we *do* 'change our educational priorities' and that the Tinas do not get left out but are prepared adequately for the world in which they will, with a bit of luck, eventually find employment. We have already pointed to the dangers of the production of a computer-educated élite and nowhere is this potentially more serious than in the field of the use of the computer as an instrument for composition, if we are at all right in our assumption that this particular technological revolution has potentially changed the nature of the writing process more decisively than anything since the invention of Gutenberg's moveable type.

Along with the more sophisticated aspects of composition can go also the possibilities of the provision of assistance in the more limited areas of skills development. Programs already exist that will help with spelling, some that come ready-made with a large vocabulary and which are capable of having their spelling vocabulary expanded. Such programs can be used as a self-checking process for the young writer and can clearly be used for remedial work both in terms of diagnosis and improvement. Sharples refers to a program described by Pain in *Proceedings of IFIP 3rd World Conference on Computers in Education,*[17] which provides a computer aid for spelling error classification in remedial teaching. It contains a simple parser which recognizes some correctly spelt words that are used wrongly in context ('their' in the phrase 'Once there' in the example below):

> STORY: *Once their was a prety princess who*
>
> xxxxxxxxxxxxxxxxxxxxxxxxxxxxxxxxxxxxxxxxxxxxxxxxxxxxxxxxxxxxxxxxxxxxx
>
> SPELLING CHECK: Once THEIR was a PRETY PRINCESS who
> (spelling monitor interrupts typing of story)
>
> THEIR means 'belonging to them'. Should the word be THERE meaning
> 'in that place'? *Yes*
>
> Should PRETY be PRETTY meaning 'beautiful'? *Yes*
>
> Alter the story by typing the correct words:
>
> xxxxxxxxxxxxxxxxxxxxxxxxxxxxxxxxxxxxxxxxxxxxxxxxxxxxxxxxxxxxxxxxxxxxx
>
> STORY: Once *there* was a *pretty princess* who . . .
> (computer types out the story so far, apart from words misspelt)
>
> STORY: *lived all alone. . .*
>
> (Sharples)[18]

Of course, as well as providing instant and unobtrusive help in this way, the computer can also store the errors that the student has made and provide the teacher with an accurate account and analysis of these so that this can be used as a basis for further possible remedial teaching in a later session. But the distinctive feature about the program just described seems to us to be that the student is still in command of what is going on in the production of his text. The computer 'prompts' by asking questions but, in the end, it is the student who makes the necessary decisions. This is far removed from some other programs we have seen, especially in the United States, which claim to 'individualise basic skills' and which break skills development down into a series of drill exercises, making the student subservient to the machine, which then 'reports' on his progress to the teacher. It is more than a matter of simply being 'user-friendly'; it seems to us important in the final analysis that the student remains in charge of what is going on and that he never becomes a mere slave to the machine.

This becomes even more important when we move from a relatively simple area such as spelling to the much more complex ones of punctuation, style and grammar. Here again group work may come into its own. We can envisage programs in the future which (like embryo word processors) will encourage students to play around with various ways of arranging words and in this way to realize the creative potential of the English language system, to try things out and see how they work. It may be that some of the theoretical ideas in such important books as John Keen's *Teaching English: A Linguistic Approach*[19] and Doughty, Pearce and Thornton's *Language in Use*[20] may, through well-designed computer programs, at last become accessible to the classroom teacher of English.

There are, of course, all manner of already existing language teaching techniques that can be enhanced by the use of the computer as a machine capable of manipulating text. We can immediately envisage applications in terms of the use of 'cloze procedure' and 'sequencing' exercises for example. In all of these the potential of the computer to focus attention, direct group work, and provide self-checking procedures can easily be adapted.

The reference to the 'user-friendly' aspect of the computer program is not a merely conventional one. One of the earliest applications of computers to education in this country was in Glasgow where there were experiments in using computers to help with remedial reading for adolescents. There is no doubt that, if you are having difficulty in acquiring a skill that most of your peers take for granted, it is less threatening to expose your ignorance and difficulty to a machine at times than to a living teacher. (In the same way we are told that the use of computers in medical diagnosis results in greater truth from patients in the taking of case histories. You are less likely to lie to a machine than to a living doctor about your smoking and drinking habits!) In short, if we believe that there is a continuing place for some kind of drills instruction and practice in the language arts curriculum, there is very good reason for supposing that the microcomputer can be an effective means towards this being much more intelligently, because more individually, operated upon than through the use of any 'basic skills' workbook. Jones, commenting from the perspective of a Head Teacher of an infant and junior school, makes the point very well:

> Infant teachers, in particular, have found that pre-reading skills, vocabulary checks, letter-matching, word matching, letter and sound recognition, word order, etc., have been revitalised using the computer in a CAL [computer-assisted learning] situation, especially where a drill sequence is required . . . These are many areas within the language skills curriculum that lend themselves to the application of CAL — areas, for example, that call for sequencing (often a difficult area for middle juniors), for spelling — indeed, anywhere that drills need to be established, exercised and tested *at the pace of the learner*. Children can be encouraged to work on a weakness, for such is the compulsive power of the computer, *providing, of course, that it has been properly programmed.* (our italics)[21]

We have been critical elsewhere in this book of many applications of computer-assisted learning and, at its worst, it represents all that many Language Arts teachers find most dispiriting and threatening about the use of the new technology in the classroom. Certainly this is the danger of seeing the microcomputer as a kind of more sophisticated language laboratory such as we were once familiar with in the teaching of modern languages. There are real dangers of this happening. The potentiality of computers for being linked in 'networks' (often called 'econets') so that one major computer can service and provide programs for a whole set of other 'outstation' computers is of considerable importance but contains many dangers. Using an econet arrangement, the teacher can provide individual programmed drills to students working at their own terminal, see on his own monitor screen what is happening on any terminal he chooses, and obtain detailed print-out information about each student's attainment and difficulties. Indeed, in most respects, there is no need for the teacher to be there at all. The whole thing can be left to the computer program and the motivating power of the computer terminal itself. We have seen such a system operating in a large American city. A centrally based main-frame computer provided drill instruction in a whole range of curriculum areas, including language arts and mathematics, at a variety of levels for students throughout the system. The dangers here, educationally, seem to us exactly the same as those of the language laboratory, itself hailed in its day as a means of individualizing instruction. The motivating power soon wears off and there is little evidence of the ability of students to transfer from the 'laboratory' situation to the real life one. Our own experience of trying out a computerized laboratory program of this kind was illuminating. One of us had been spending about a month in French Canada, speaking moderately good French virtually every day, but was completely floored by a 'user friendly' program on the use of the conditional tense. Indeed, the 'friendliness' became somewhat suspect when the enquiry appeared on the screen whether, in view of the number of mistakes that had been made, we would like to transfer to an easier program! Needless to say, the kind of program involved was one of the 'gap filling' kind, presenting the decontextualized language that is typical of many workbook approaches to language teaching. There is at present a large growth industry which consists of taking bad textbook exercises and turning them into equally bad computer programs. Indeed we have noted a number of them already in this book.

There may, as with the language laboratory, be a place for this kind of thing within very specialized contexts. Research on the effectiveness of this kind of teaching shows that, for highly motivated adults working for clearly defined and very limited goals (learning enough Japanese to enable you to communicate with salesmen in your own specialist field before going on a promotional tour of Japan, for example), such teaching methods can be very effective. It remains doubtful, however, how much of this kind of learning stays with the learner once the immediate occasion for its use has worn off. *The Effective Use of Reading*[22] showed, much to the dismay of some specialists in the field, that even SRA reading laboratories, *when they were used as part of a carefully planned and total programme of remedial reading instruction* could produce observable gains in children using them. But, of course, the real danger of reading laboratories is that they can equally be misused (and frequently are) so that they become a *substitute* for a properly designed and total programme of instruction. But, because the potential for misuse is there and we can see plenty of examples of it in operation in classrooms, we ought not to allow this to blind us to the potential effective use of drill techniques and programs. As we have stressed throughout the previous pages, the introduction of the microcomputer into the classroom raises primarily management questions and, in this case, *the management of the learning*, how we relate the drills to the rest of the learning that is going on, becomes of crucial importance. There is a useful collection of articles in *Exploring English with Microcomputers*,[23] edited by Chandler, published by the Council for Educational Technology on the occasion of the Easter 1983 conference of the National Association for the Teaching of English. In this, most of the contributors stress the importance of seeing the microcomputer as an adjunct to already good English teaching already going on, not as something that can exist and work wonders in its own right. But, as suggested earlier, the insights into language that well-designed programs can provide is potentially significant. Here the possibility of extending the range of options available to the teacher is of the first importance. Given the nature of first degree courses in English in most British universities many teachers of the subject are woefully ill-equipped in their knowledge of language and present-day approaches to grammar. A consequence is that, now that old fashioned grammar teaching ('tradgram' as it is often dismissively called) is discredited, there is an enormous vacuum in this area of the curriculum. What kind of language study should we be engaged in? How do we make up for the deficiencies in the *teacher's* knowledge of language so that some worthwhile work in this area can be done by the pupils? Programmes such as the BBC Radio series, *Web of Language* (now available as a book with supporting cassettes, Oxford, 1982) and INSET materials such as the Open University Post Experience course on *Language Development* have done a good deal to help but there is still much to be accomplished in this area. Here the work of Mike Sharples, already extensively referred to, and reported in Chandler (1983), seems likely to be especially significant. Sharples is currently working on the potential of a 'language workshop' with the microcomputer as a kind of construction kit for language so that his workshop has:

> . . . the same general function and components as a carpentry workshop: a set of tools, to explore, construct and modify text; a stockpile of useful linguistic parts such as definitions and synonyms; a detailed instruction manual describing the function of each tool and a *Teach Yourself* Guide suggesting games, exercises and projects in story building. (Sharples)[24]

With such a workshop the student can be encouraged to manipulate text according to the principles of transformational grammar and teachers, who may themselves have very little linguistic knowledge, can become co-explorers alongside their students. With the software that he is currently developing we may be on the threshold of a new opportunity both to teach linguistic understanding and to put that understanding to use in genuinely creative contexts. Sharples points out that neither Latinate grammar teaching nor the study of literature alone has done much to help a pupil to write coherent and fluent essays. His expectation is that the use of the microcomputer in language teaching can assist a planned programme of language development, which will help the student to make more consciously informed choices about the way in which language is being used in writing:

> The findings of contemporary research in psychology and linguistics have not been widely applied to teaching. They suggest that if a child is to develop her writing in a controlled manner she must learn to plan a story form, to create text suited to audience and function and to understand and manipulate the structures of language. An exceptional scheme which includes these ideas is 'Language in Use'. Based on modern descriptive linguistics, 'Language in Use' encourages the pupil to explore the structure of language by, for example, playing with word order, writing advertising copy or inventing nonsense words. The pupil's linguistic knowledge is applied to creative writing through controlled composition exercises.

He rightly points out that *Language in Use* has failed to obtain wide acceptance in the classroom. Indeed, it has been called one of the most widely sold and least used books on English teaching. Its main problem, as its authors would now probably acknowledge, was that it assumed too much willingness on the part of teachers both to develop their own linguistic knowledge and to develop the necessary classroom materials. *Language in Use* looks like a set of ready-made materials for the classroom but does, in fact, demand a great deal of work and adaptation of its ideas by the teacher before they can be made workable. This is where the microcomputer might come in:

> Until now there have been no facilities for children to easily generate sentences from a grammar; add syntactic and semantic constraints; discover the effects of simple transformational rules; explore alternative story styles; quickly access composing aids, such as a thesaurus. Natural language computer programs can offer just such a 'language workshop' which, alongside written worksheets, could expose a child's intuitive knowledge of language and, by addressing issues of style rather than correctness, use it to extend his skills of creative writing.

The possibilities suggested here seem of great significance. Much work was done on the theoretical aspects of language and English teaching in the sixties; indeed *Language in Use* was itself the product of such work, an attempt to apply the insights of Halliday's grammar to classroom English teaching. From the work of Britton[25] and others a good deal has been learned about the relationship between style and the function and audience for which a piece of writing is intended. The problem comes when we try to find ways of teaching which will enable theoretical understanding about language to affect the way in which students actually write. Now the ability to manipulate language that the microcomputer provides, the exploration of both natural language and computer language by the student, joined with the potential of the computer functioning as a word processor, may enable much more conscious language development to take place than has ever been possible before. We may be on the threshold of actually *knowing* how to help students to develop their mastery of language rather than leaving it to a purely *ad hoc, intuitive* process as now. At present when students do learn to write effectively current methods of English teaching seem sound enough; unfortunately we all have to recognize that this is a very hit and miss business. The surveys conducted by the Assessment of Performance Unit have shown that in the area of 'basic literacy' the schools are doing well enough. It is in the much more difficult areas of suiting style to content, appreciating the use of different registers, being positively aware of style and stylistic choice, that the performance of school leavers seems to be wanting. If Sharples and his co-workers are right in their hopes we may be on the brink of changing this and enabling English teachers, and other teachers in and through language, to become more technically skilled in teaching a mastery of the craft of writing.

There will be those, of course, who will claim that to place such stress on 'mastery' will take away the 'mystery' (or mystique) that underlies much English teaching. Similar points were made at the time of Gutenberg about the effects of printing upon the production of illuminated manuscripts. The point is that if English teaching is to survive the impact of 'Gutenberg Two' it will have to learn to adapt to the conditions of life in the world that is so speedily evolving. Books are not, of course, going to become obsolete; they remain a potent source of pleasure as well as information. But, as Chandler has suggested, 'tapping it out' is likely to be a more common resort in many situations than 'looking it up'. Alongside the traditional literacy skills, therefore, we shall certainly need to acquire and teach new skills such as the use of the keyboard and the ability to read a screen. There is already some evidence, too, that the new technology is actually changing the way in which we communicate. The shape and size of the screen places a certain premium on succinct and economical language use. Layout and organization of material take on a new significance. So far too little thinking seems to have been done about the effects of technology on linguistic change. Yet, by an almost unnoticed revolution (except by a few English teachers seeking to hold back the inevitability of change), the development of the electric typewriter has transformed the stylistic conventions which underlie the writing of letters and reports and this, in its turn, has had its effect on printing styles and conventions. The increased use of computer-type print-out display in both advertising and television suggests that a similar change is taking place at the present time. When *The Hitch Hikers' Guide to the Galaxy* was adapted for television the 'computer print-out' subtitles were part of the sci-fi jokiness with which the series was concerned; now, a year or so later, we take them for granted when they appear on our screen. We are unlikely to see a return to the traditional teaching of précis in our schools since the conditions which made the teaching of précis of value have now disappeared. However, new conditions do mean that we shall certainly have to teach students how to organize information logically and how to express ideas (and probably feelings also) concisely and within the boundaries of the 'frame' provided by a visual display. Until recently schools have been slow to adapt to changing conditions: we went on teaching logarithms long after the invention of the pocket calculator, for example. If schools are not to become increasingly irrelevant to the changing society that we explored in an earlier chapter they will have to adapt very urgently to the new 'literacy' needs in a computerized age.

   This will certainly entail a much greater awareness of the importance of 'graphicacy' skills in communication. Not only is there the organization of the words within the frame to be attended to and the consideration of the impact that they are likely to make visually as well as literally; there is also, through the use of computer graphics and colour presentation, a whole series of new communication techniques available through the use of the visual language of film and television, the use of wipes, fades and dissolves for example. The growth of television advertising produced a generation which was much more visually sophisticated than ever before and this is likely to be even more the case when students have had the opportunity to experiment with their own computer graphics at home.

There is one further area in which teachers of the Language Arts, especially in the context of English studies, ought to take note of microelectronics and computers. If an understanding of the role of microelectronics in society of the kind we argue for in the following chapter is to operate at a more than cognitive level, some note ought also to be taken of the ever-increasing body of imaginative literature in this area. Indeed, we may see the treatment of matters of this kind as going back a long way, long before the machines were themselves invented. It was Chandler in an early lecture delivered to the Bryanston Seminar who first drew our attention to the treatment, in a satirical manner, by Swift of something very like a Turing machine, such as we described earlier. The title of Chandler's lecture was 'Living in Lagado', since published by the MEP, and he opened by drawing upon Swift's account of the Grand Academy, published in *Gulliver's Travels* in 1726, but certainly written much earlier.

Gulliver is taken on a tour of the Grand Academy in the capital city of the Island of Laputa where there are innumerable Professors at work on highly speculative projects designed to bring happiness to mankind. Here Gulliver sees a machine resembling more a 'mainframe' computer than a microcomputer, and this must be supposed to be the first appearance in literature of something looking very like a computer. It is worth quoting the extract in full:

THE first Professor I saw was in a very large Room, with Forty Pupils about him. After Salutation, observing me to look earnestly upon a Frame, which took up the greatest part of both the Length and Breadth of the Room; he said, perhaps I might wonder to see him employed in a Project for improving speculative Knowledge by practical and mechanical Operations. But the World would soon be sensible of its Usefulness; and he flattered himself, that a more noble exalted Thought never sprang in any other Man's Head. Every one knew how laborious the usual Method is of attaining to Arts and Sciences; whereas by his Contrivance, the most ignorant Person at a reasonable Charge, and with a little bodily Labour, may write Books in Philosophy, Poetry, Politicks, Law, Mathematicks and Theology, without the least Assistance from Genius or Study. He then led me to the Frame, about the Sides whereof all his Pupils stood in Ranks. It was Twenty Foot square, placed in the Middle of the Room. The Superficies was composed of several Bits of Wood, about the Bignes of a Dye, but some larger than others. They were all linked together by slender Wires. These Bits of Wood were covered on every Square with Papers pasted on them; and on these Papers were written all the Words of their Language; in their several Moods, Tenses, and Declensions, but without any Order. The Professor then desired me to observe, for he was going to set his Engine at work. The Pupils at his Command took each of them hold of an Iron Handle, whereof there were Forty fixed round the Edges of the Frame; and giving them a sudden Turn, the whole Disposition of the Words was entirely changed. He then commanded Six and Thirty of the Lads to read the several Lines softly as they appeared upon the Frame; and where they found three or four Words together that might make Part of a Sentence, they dictated to the four remaining Boys who were Scribes. This Work was repeated three or four Times, and at every Turn the Engine was so contrived, that the Words shifted into new Places, as the square Bits of Wood moved upside down.

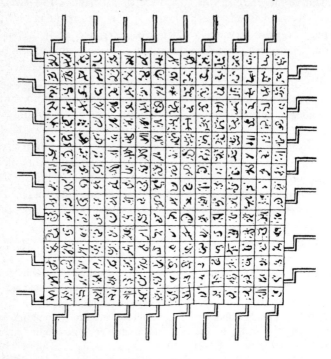

Six Hours a-Day the young Students were employed in this Labour; and the Professor shewed me several volumes in large Folio already collected, of broken Sentences, which he intended to piece together; and out of those rich Materials to give the World a compleat Body of all Arts and Sciences; which however might be still improved, and much expedited, if the Publick would raise a Fund for making and employing five Hundred such Frames in *Lagado,* and oblige the Managers to contribute in common their several Collections.

HE assured me, that this Invention had employed all his Thoughts from his Youth; that he had emptied the whole Vocabulary into his Frame, and made the strictest Computation of the general Proportion there is in Books between the Number of Particles, Nouns, and Verbs, and other Parts of Speech.

I MADE my humblest Acknowledgements to this illustrious Person for his great Communicativeness; and promised if ever I had the good Fortune to return to my native Country, that I would do him Justice, as the sole Inventor of this wonderful Machine; the Form and Contrivance of which I desired Leave to delineate upon Paper as in the Figure here annexed. I told him, although it were the custom of our Learned in *Europe* to steal Inventions from each other, who had thereby at least this Advantage, that it became a Controversy which was the right Owner; yet I would take such Caution, that he should have the Honour entire without a Rival. [26]

What is interesting about this is not just Swift's prescience, which is remarkable enough by all means, but the assumption that a machine such as this would be bound to produce nothing but nonsense. One of the authors remembers early experiments in machine translation which might have been based almost exactly on this description from Swift and language experts who regarded the whole enterprise with a scorn and scepticism equivalent to that of Swift even if expressed with less *saeva indignatio*. On the whole, until relatively recently, this is fairly typical of the treatment of the microprocessor in literature. It is usually seen as in some way a threat to humanity, something that needs to be controlled at all costs. Certainly the concept of the 'user-friendly' machine is not one that occurs to most writers. Specialists in the field of science fiction, and one supposes that 'computer literature' must be re-garded as a sub-branch of this well-established genre, have coined the term 'the Frankenstein Complex', the assumption by most writers about modern machines that they are a danger to traditional ways of life, lurking and ready to take over the world if we do not contain them very carefully. There is a long tradition in English literature of mistrust of innovation; most utopias turn in the end into dystopias, and it is arguable that this is one of the influences that makes the arts-based graduate both impatient and suspicious of many of the issues raised in this book. Our own work with English teachers suggests that many of them have an initial hostility to the use of microprocessors in their classrooms either in the form of computers or of word processors, and this hostility based upon ignorance and fear, is one manifestation of the Franken-stein Complex.

Isaac Asimov, who has written frequently and well about the development of intelligent machines, 'robots', describes in the sequence of stories contained in the two collections *I, Robot*[27] and *The Rest of the Robots*[28] how, as 'U.S. Robots' becomes a multinational corporation engaged in the manufacture and supply of 'mechanical men', humanity insisted on built-in devices to ensure that the robots could not harm mankind. Hence Asimov came to develop what he called 'The Three Laws of Robotics', designed to be placed in all robot brains and to which all other elements of their design would be subsidiary.

The now well-known Laws are:

1. A robot may not injure a human being, or, through inaction, allow
    a human being to come to harm.

2. A robot must obey the orders given it by human beings except
    where such orders would conflict with the First Law.
3. A robot must protect its own existence as long as such protection
    does not conflict with the First or Second Law.

These 'Laws' were first stated explicitly in a robot story entitled
'Runaround', first published in 1941 and included in *I, Robot*, and have
gained wide currency since. Indeed, Asimov himself comments that 'many
writers of robot stories, without actually quoting the three laws, take them for
granted and expect the readers to do the same.' He continues wryly:

> In fact I have been told that if, in future years, I am to be remembered at all,
> it will be for these three laws of robotics. In a way this bothers me, for I am
> accustomed to thinking of myself as a scientist, and to be remembered for the
> non-existent basis of a non-existent science is embarrassing. Yet if robotics
> ever does reach the pitch of excellence described in my stories, it may be that
> something like the Three Laws will really come into existence and, if so, I
> will have achieved a rather unusual (if, alas, posthumous) triumph.

Asimov has written a few stories directly about computers and computers
appear inevitably a good deal elsewhere in his science fiction writing but it is
in the robot stories that much of his writing of relevance to exploring computers in literature will be found in spite of their titles. An important critical
study by Joseph Patrouch makes the point:

> Asimov seems to consider the difference between a robot and a computer to
> be primarily a matter of mobility, which he takes to be a nondefinitive differ-
> ence, so that he refuses to distinguish between the two. This means that any
> Asimov computer story could also be considered an Asimov Robot story.[29]

Teachers seeking stories by Asimov explicitly about computers would,
however, find it useful to look at 'The Last Question' (in *Opus 100*),[30]
'Escape!' and 'The Evitable Conflict' (both in *I, Robot*),[31] as well as the
well-known, 'The Fun They Had' (most easily accessible in *The Best of Isaac
Asimov*,)[32] which was first written in 1954. In this excellent *very* short story
the theme is education: the 'home teacher' has broken down (interestingly the
home-teaching computer sets homework, gives tests and teaches vulgar fractions — reminding us of Papert's comments on the limited educational purposes to which we are often putting the new machines) and the two children
turn to an old book they find lying about neglected in the house. The year is
2157 and, as the children turn the pages, they are struck by their strangeness:

> It was awfully funny to read words that stood still instead of moving the way
> they were supposed to — on a screen, you know. And then, when they turned
> back to the page before, it had the same words on it that it had had when they
> read it for the first time.

At the end of the story the computer is repaired, the screen lights up, the fractions come back, and one of the children, Margie, is left sighing:

> She was thinking about the old schools they had when her grandfather's
> grandfather was a little boy. All the kids from the whole neighbourhood
> came, laughing and shouting in the schoolyard, sitting together in the
> schoolroom, going home together at the end of the day. They learned the
> same things, so they could help each other on the homework and talk about
> it . . . Margie was thinking about how the kids must have loved it in the old
> days. She was thinking about the fun they had.

There is a good deal here that would repay discussion with an English class
and a good deal too of sound educational thinking. In the *Times Educational
Supplement* (2 October 1981) Dale Suttleworth,[33] who was responsible for ten
years for the development of a system of alternative schools under the Toronto
Board of Education, wrote:

> Unless we change our schools, we shall soon be bypassed. IBM and
> Westinghouse have plenty of programs coming along to 'educate' kids. The
> 'content' side of education can be provided on videotape and education can
> be provided on videotape and by computer. If the schools don't change, less
> and less money will be voted to the state school system — and commercial
> interests — possibly through the voucher system — will dominate the edu-
> cation of the future. Until teachers realise that they have to become masters
> of process — how you learn, how you relate to others — and are seen to be ex-
> pert in this, a takeover of education by big business will remain a danger.

We believe that issues such as this, which receive further treatment in the
following chapter, ought to be discussed in classrooms and that the expression
of the consequences of certain tendencies in society as explored in imaginative
literature is one of the best ways of enabling students to have some awareness
and understanding of the choices we have to make about how we want to live
in the future.

The classic treatment of the computer in literature in English is, of course,
in E. M. Forster's *The Machine Stops*,[34] also a remarkably prescient piece of
work. Like so much else of its period it has a concern about a life dependent
upon machines leading to a cocooned life isolating people from direct experience. When the machine, unthinkably, breaks down, mankind finds itself
unable to survive, though there is some hope residing in those 'Homeless' who
have lived outside the machine all along:

> 'But, Kuno, is is true? Are there still men on the surface of the earth? Is this
> — this tunnel, this poisoned darkness — really not the end?'
>
> He replied:
>
> 'I have seen them, spoken to them, loved them. They are hiding in the mist
> and the ferns until our civilization stops. To-day they are the Homeless — to-
> morrow — '

'Oh, to-morrow — some fool will start the Machine again, to-morrow.'

'Never', said Kuno, 'never. Humanity has learnt its lesson.'

As he spoke the whole city was broken like a honeycomb. An air-ship had sailed in through the vomitory into a ruined wharf. It crashed downwards, exploding as it went, rending gallery after gallery with its wings of steel. For a moment they saw the nations of the dead, and, before they joined them, scraps of the untainted sky.

On the whole the machine has not had a very good press, and until recently a Luddite attitude has dominated its treatment in our literature. It comes as something of a relief to find more positive attitudes beginning to develop and more 'user-friendly' machines beginning to appear. Perhaps the beginnings of this change of mood are to be seen in the highly entertaining computer, H A L, in the film *2001*, and recently Laurence Lerner has written two amusing and thought-provoking sequences of poems, *ARTHUR: The Life and Opinions of a Digital Computer* [35] and *ARTHUR and MARTHA: Or, the Loves of the Computers*. [36] It is to be hoped, and expected, that there will be more literature with this positive note in the future. Certainly in those departments where the teaching of English is organized on thematic lines there would be a clear place for a unit on the treatment of computers and other forms of microelectronics in literature. Such treatment would also find a place in integrated programmes in humanities teaching such as we discuss briefly in Chapter 8. Currently Adams and Chandler are working on an anthology which will collect together the ways in which the computer has figured in imaginative writing and its publication should make accessible a good deal of material difficult to come by at the present time.

There are a multitude of futures still possible for us. An education in the Language Arts should not just give students the necessary skills and capacities to survive in that world of the future; it should also give them imaginative understanding that will enable them to play their part in forming and determining the nature of the future that evolves. This is one reason why we felt that it was necessary to write a book arguing the central role of the teacher of the humanities in thinking and teaching about society and microelectronics. We neglect that role at our peril.

7

Microelectronics and Social Studies

Not all schools have a timetable slot labelled Social Studies. There are still some secondary schools that make no provision at all for the study of our own society and how it works, though presumably issues may be considered in the course of work on History or Geography or even Home Economics. This patchy coverage is reflected in the absence of any kind of Social Studies paper among the syllabuses of some of our CSE Boards. It is astonishing that schools can limit themselves in this way when we so obviously live in a fast-changing, difficult and dangerous world. Our children desparately need an understanding of their world, their community, the context of their own lives, if they are to have any hope of securing a measure of control over their own destinies. It is partly the argument of this chapter that the enormously rapid and powerful developments in microelectronics greatly reinforce the need for schools to come to grips with Social Studies.

When Boards do offer examinations in Social Studies, one is impressed very often by the breadth of the coverage and one wonders if there is ever time during the school week to look at any issue in depth. Certainly, the issues with which we are concerned in this book and which we discussed in Chapters 2 and 4 tend to get brief mention, it at all. Yet how can a modern Social Studies course have serious relevance to young people if it does not spend time thinking about the impact of technological change in a world of changing power structures and social tensions? We are dealing with the daily lives and aspirations of us all.

Schools do suffer from the pressure of conflicting demands on their syllabuses. Many would do more to help their pupils develop the skills, among others, that we discuss in this book were it not for the necessity to prepare them for public examinations and the qualifications that might make the difference between being skilled or unskilled in a society with increasingly little use for the latter. They might do more if there were not so much ill-informed pressure for a return to 'basics' and the traditional 'subjects' (this latter from the current political leadership of the Department of Education and Science who, at the same time, are supposed to be supporting the Microelectronic

Education Programme; no wonder the Department is bypassed by other Ministries where there is slightly more awareness of national need in educational terms).

There are some examination syllabuses that provide for work on the social implications of the 'new technology'. These are the syllabuses in Computer Studies, which have seen a very rapid growth in recent years. Even so, Computer Studies remains very clearly a minority subject, an option among other options. A look at the syllabuses makes it clear why this is so. They are, without exception, largely technical. They involve, whether it is a CSE or a GCE 'O'-level syllabus, a study of the principles of the hardware and of programming. There is technically slanted work on applications; many Boards provide opportunities for candidates to write simple programs as course work. There is a study of systems analysis, data processing and computer languages. Then, finally, there is some very slight attention to implications.

Here are two not untypical examples. Section 7 of the North Regional Examinations Board (NREB) provides the following:

> Candidates should be able to:
> 7.1   describe the social changes which have occurred as a result of developments in computing;
> 7.2   describe the possible effects of computers on employment;
> 7.3   describe applications of data banks in three particular fields;
> 7.4   recall some ways in which society benefits from the use of data banks;
> 7.5   recall some dangers which are inherent in the use of computers to manage files of personal data;
> 7.6   describe the safeguards which are necessary to prevent possible misuse of data banks: accuracy and updating, security, limitations on use, notification of existence, compulsory disclosure and right of appeal.

Perhaps the stress on data safeguards is no bad thing in a country which has, as yet, not legislated in terms of the European Convention on the matter (and is losing business as a consequence). It seems unlikely that too much school time will be spent on the topic (let alone 7.2!) as Section 7 as a whole is worth exactly 9% of the total marks for the examination.

The Metropolitan Regional Examinations Board (commonly thought of as being a somewhat 'progressive' board) has this to offer:

> (c)   Implications and/or Applications (Project)
>
> A project concerning the implications and/or applications of computers should be presented. The project must not include practical programming. (Note: provided in Section (a)). A suggested list of topics for this section is given below but must not be regarded as exclusive.

> A case history of a local (real or imaginary) firm that has installed
> a computer, the changes that it has caused in the firm, the money
> it has cost or saved and how the employees reacted.
> Data banks — security, privacy and the need for protective
> legislation.
> The use of computer systems in a particular field, e.g. banking,
> medicine, traffic control, electricity and gas billing, licensing.
> Process control.
> Description of a real time computer application.

These options seem a good deal more specific than the generalities of the NREB syllabus and no doubt a student tackling, for example, the first of the suggestions could make very good use of the opportunity. Even so, it is clearly possible for students to take this examination course without giving one single thought to the social implications. In the examination, the project is worth 15% of the total marks.

Remember that Computer Studies are taken only by a minority of our examination candidates — because of their technical nature. The courses are inevitably seen as vocationally biased, as opening up the possibility for some kind of a career with computers.

In the meantime, the majority, in many schools, have little opportunity to consider the impact of the computers on their own lives, let alone have any experience of using one of the machines. As everyone knows, the Department of Industry has financed half of the cost of a micro for all secondary schools and is now in the process of doing the same for primary schools. One wonders where they are and for what they are used. There will be far too many stuck permanently in a computer room in the Maths Department occupied by the Computer Studies Group or sixth form computer buffs.

One must not be too unfair. As we have seen, and will continue to see as the book progresses, there are schools which take a much broader view of how their computer is to be used. The Microelectronics Education Programme is clearly anxious that machines should not be the preserve of Computer Studies — though its thinking remains, in our view, still too technically oriented. *Computers in Schools* (the journal of MUSE – Microcomputer Users in Education) may just occasionally have articles touching on the Humanities among the numbers of those dealing with work in maths and science or with technical issues. There is a sharp contrast here with the journal produced by MAPE (*Microcomputers and Primary Education*). This is much more lively, much more aware of children and the classroom, much less limited by technical considerations — though sound technical help is given. We would argue that membership of MAPE is a much better 'buy' for the secondary Humanities teacher than MUSE — though there is much to be said for helping MUSE to broaden its outlook.

There are two issues here which seem to us to be of major importance. First, there is a danger that the pattern of Computer Studies centred in Maths or Science, together with, in many cases, 'club' activities for a few eager spirits hooked on programming, can lead to the development of a school computer élite. They will have no difficulty in developing their own language! School élites of this kind lead inexorably to élites in society at large. The computer élite is unlikely to hold (or seek?) political power directly, but it could have control over electronic technology as it develops and act very much as 'gatekeeper' filtering through to the uninitiated masses only what is good for them. The Orwellian version in *Nineteen Eighty Four*[1] could be made more likely if education takes the wrong turning.

We argue with a degree of passion that all our children need to understand and be able to make use of the technology. We want a generation so educated that they cannot be prevented from having full and equal access to the information stocks of our society.

The second issue follows directly from the first. We are advocating the widest possible acquaintance with the technology. We are arguing that computers can be seen at their best advantage if they are used imaginatively in Humanities work. To utilize the strengths of this flexible teaching aid in English, in History, in Geography, in Religious Education, is to contribute to that general ease and familiarity that we believe is vital in our democracy. There remains, however, special responsibilities upon the shoulders of the teachers in schools who deal with the Social Studies area of the curriculum. This chapter will, then, discuss how Social Studies teaching can play its part in developing the necessary awareness and understanding as well as suggesting specific uses of the computer as a teaching aid.

Computer Awareness

Today's children are growing up in a world of electronics. The work that is already starting in a variety of junior schools shows how easily children adapt to the machines and what creative use they can make of them. The preceding chapters have given something of the flavour of this work and its potential for teaching. More urgent is the provision of the right kind of help to older secondary pupils. A great deal is happening or planned in terms of the education, or training, of the 14–17 age group and it seems to us of the highest importance that we get it right.

We have already noted some of the obstacles. The present examination pattern at 16+ is obsolescent yet it seems almost impossible to hasten the birth of a single school leaving examination for 16-year-olds. As one looks at the reports of the various working parties set up by the Boards and the comments and alternative plans that have emerged from the dying Schools Council, and as one considers the conservatism in the profession and the Department of

Education and Science, there is inevitable anxiety that, new examination or not, courses in schools will continue on much the same lines, with much the same subjects.

Then, in 1983, we shall see the emergence of what could be an alternative school system — the New Training Initiative (NTI). The pilot scheme involves a number of providers. There are co-operating Local Education Authorities who will be providing facilities for NTI courses in colleges and schools. Other courses will be run in the Training Departments of large companies. The courses will be run under the control of the Manpower Services Commission (MSC). That is, the curriculum will be decided within the MSC. It is intended that 30% of the time in these courses will be devoted to technical or vocational training. It seems that, during the remainder of the time, there will be a good deal of attention focused on what are now curiously called 'Life Skills'. These would seem to include basic literacy and numeracy as well as an introduction to the institutions of the country and how they function, together with help on such matters as job getting, adaptation to work and, possibly, leisure pursuits. It is intended that courses should be wholly non-political.

There are already some anxieties about this. It is suggested that one course has had support withdrawn because it encouraged young people to canvass popular ideas about unemployment and its causes. In fact, there are educationists of standing on the MSC Steering Committee for the Initiative and the sheer pressure of needs will necessitate the heavy involvement of teachers all over the country. In other words, there are great opportunities but the Initiative will need watching. It is vital that the educational component of these courses encourages young people to become self-reliant and critical.

As we write, the situation is confused. Certainly, government Departments, other than that of Education and Science, are becoming increasingly involved in education (through the side door of training) and this is partly the consequence of weaknesses in the DES itself. If it is true that the MSC initiative will lead to major changes in the education of young people, then the Humanities must stake its claim. It will do so if it is clear about objectives and if teachers of the Humanities are properly aware of both the dangers and potential of the new technology in our society.

There can be no doubt whatever of the impact of microelectronics on employment and our way of life. Though a good deal of current unemployment, as we have noted, is a consequence of the British version of depression, a good deal is also structural. There is a major industrial shift in process. Decisions or non-decisions taken by youngsters today will have a profound effect on their lives. As a recent article by Alex Hamilton in the *Observer* (19 December 1982)[2] noted, there is now even some reduction in the size of the labour force in the computer industry while the long period of increase in service employment in both public and private sectors has halted.

Most worrying of all, the advent of the 'information revolution' in microcomputers and communication is threatening jobs in the service sector as dramatically as robotics is doing in the traditional manufacturing processes. The clerical jobs in expanding financial services and the Civil Service fields are the very ones which the mini-computer at your elbow can most readily replace.

The article goes on to note: 'There is a real and pernicious danger that the end result would be the division of countries into two nations, a highly paid, highly skilled group at the top, and a low-paid, low and unskilled majority at the bottom.' In the light of this comment, our earlier reference to Orwell may seem even more apposite for, indeed, there are frightening political implications in such a trend. The *Observer* journalist goes on, as many writers have in the last few years, to insist that structural change is inevitable and should be encouraged and invested in, while at the same time: 'Society should encourage a wider range of people to work more flexibly in ways that can occur with new technology and the decline of traditional factory or office working.' If Alex Hamilton is right (together with others who say much the same) then there is a very heavy responsibility laid on the education system. It is not just a matter of teaching 'Life Skills' and turning out 'adaptable' young people, it is a matter of preparing young people who can think, question, understand and act.

Humanities (and, in this context, Social Studies) has two important tasks. First of all, it must contribute to the acquisition of skills; secondly, it must ensure that young people are aware of the changes that are taking place, how they affect them and what they might be able to do about it.

What is being done so far? *Educational Computing* in February 1981 published a report from a school in the north of England that was running a course for *all* pupils in one term of the third year. The course in Computer Education takes one double period (70 minutes) a week. Here is the outline of the twelve lesson course:

1. A system of storing and retrieving information
2. A means of manipulating data very rapidly
3. A means of trying plans and ideas
4. An aid in learning and teaching
5. A device for calculating
6. The computer as input, process, output
7. The dedicated microprocessor
8. Computers and jobs — the positive side
9. Computers and jobs — the negative side
10. Computers and leisure
11. Computers and privacy
12. Computers in action

The course involves a degree of 'hands-on' experience while the final session takes the pupils into their own locality to see 'something of how computers affect the daily working lives of people'.

The article provided a more detailed synopsis of the two lessons on employment:

8. Computers and jobs — the positive side.

    Demonstration materials: Videotape of electronic office; Kimball tapes; computerised library tickets.

    Objectives: Pupils should be aware of the following kinds of jobs in computing and the level of training and status which go with them — computer operator, computer programmer, data processing manager.

9. Computers and jobs — the negative side.

    Objectives: Pupils should know the worst and best predictions for employment in their lifetimes. They should be able to discuss the partial contribution of the microprocessor to the trend in unemployment.

    They should be able to articulate sensible answers to the questions 'Why do people work?' and 'What happens to people who are faced with being put out of work?'

All third year pupils take this course and it is clear that at the end of it they will hve a good understanding of what a computer is and what it can do. They will also appreciate that 'chip' technology is more than just computers; it involves control devices, robotics, office automation and so on; and they will have had some opportunity to think about crucial issues. As well as thinking about jobs, they will have looked at the problem of data privacy and spent a little while talking about the way the machines are going to change home life and leisure. It is possible to criticize this course; certainly, it is something of a crash course and it is a pity that it has anchored so firmly in the third year. What kinds of follow-up are there?

However, what we have here is a head-teacher rightly concerned and doing all he can within the constraints. In many schools, it would be difficult to tackle such a course later than the third year simply because of the pressure of the examination syllabuses. Our own feeling is that, if work of this sort is to be tackled with older pupils, then it must open up more discussion and must be very carefully structured to meet the perceived needs of adolescents. Ideally, we need a course for the older pupils that can build on the kind of third year course described above with its useful presentation of information appropriate to the younger age group.

We now touch on a major source of concern to social studies teachers. How are children motivated? There is plenty of evidence that young people have been 'turned off' courses in civics, for example. Equally, there is not much evidence that courses based on more modern sociological theory have been much more popular. Yet many Social Studies teachers are uneasy about the kind of course described above. It could be too prescriptive; it could fail to capture the interests of the pupils who will not see its relevance to themselves; it could be superficial.

Medway and Goodson[3] have argued persuasively that, since all learning is ultimately dependent upon the pupils' response, a syllabus planned to provide 'coverage' and 'significant' learning experiences will anyway fail if it does not (as is often the case) fire an intensely personal response from the pupil. They go on to argue, on the basis of their experience, that learning which develops from the pupils' own questions is more likely to lead to their learning what is 'important'. But the pupils, of course, have to be encouraged to raise their own questions and for this to happen teachers need the resources that can be used both to trigger off questions and then to assist in the discovery of answers. Whitby and Gleeson[4] sum up the dilemmas and indicate what we believe to be the necessary approach to the social implications of microelectronics:

> Our discussion of prevailing approaches to Social Studies teaching has, however, focussed upon two major criticisms. Firstly that, despite their pretensions to relevance, the various approaches to the subject have often seemed pointless to pupils. Secondly that, despite its frequently radical image, Social Studies teaching has often been uncritical of the society it claims to study and hence has played its part in sustaining the status quo in school and society. It is clearly our contention that, before Social Studies can generate a genuinely critical awareness of society and possibly make some contribution to social change, it must be seen by pupils to have some point.

It is hard to think of any area in life that has more point than getting a job and why this might be difficult. The difficulties do not lie with the pupils but with society itself and the decisions of government. We are deeply concerned about what seems to be the prevailing philosophy of the New Training Initiative and similar proposals. They are based, it seems to us, on a deficit theory. It is implied that young people do not find work because they are not bright enough or they lack certain skills or their langugae is inadequate or their background. . . It is a familiar list. Deficit theories of education did not work with the 'disadvantaged' in the sixties and they will not work in the eighties for they do not treat students with proper dignity or with proper respect for what they have to offer. Nevertheless, there are skills that we need to make generally available, comprehensively available, and we do need to place the learning of these skills into the kind of social studies context advocated by Gleeson and Whitby:

The Bryanston Seminar reached these conclusions:

> The microprocessor makes it possible to by-pass institutionalised education by establishing skill matching programs in which individuals articulate their own learning demands and are then, by use of the computer, linked up with someone who can fulfil those demands.

A society that depends upon the new technology could conceivably demand very different skills from its citizens than those taught in schools at present. It might well demand a greater emphasis on collective methods of working, divergent rather than convergent thinking and a refusal to take assumptions for granted.

We are not so certain about the deschooling implications (to which we return in the final chapter) but we would stress, yet again, the point about independent learning which, in fact, fits well with the second point about collective methods. The independent and personally secure learner is the better collaborator! There are clear messages here for Social Studies teaching if it is to be effective.

At the moment, it has to be said, there are very few examples of good programs available for Social Studies teaching and this is yet another indication of the currently skewed priorities. There can be no doubt that computer programs can enhance even the conventional Social Studies curriculum — and in the direction of 'collective methods of working' and 'divergent thinking'. Gleeson and Whitby, in their useful book, report two school projects that could be enhanced in this way.

In one school, pupils expressed anxiety about what they had vaguely heard about plans for their own community. The teacher's response was to produce for them two sets of figures:

Present population of the area:	14,500
Population after redevelopment:	5,750

As the teacher reported, this produced very many questions. A number of these had to be factual. In other words, pupils were faced with (1) an exercise in data collection and (2) an exercise in data interpretation as part of the task of evaluating the proposed redevelopment. They came back with, broadly, two kinds of information: (1) personal reactions from people either in the community or involved with the planning and (2) factual data about population trends, redevelopment costs, social costs, etc. These latter could have been computerized and greatly assisted the group in their questioning approach.

In the other example, a group of girls in a Bristol school made a study of hospitals. This involved them in hospital visits (including voluntary work in some of them) plus a great deal of data collection — factual information about the system and material derived from a questionnaire about the NHS which they devised and put to a sample of the general public. A computer clearly would have saved them a good deal of time in analysing the data with more time for discussion and reaching conclusions.

There are many other direct possibilities for the use of a computer program in social studies and in response to the needs of the pupils:

Educational opportunities in the neighbourhood compared with national figures.

What happens when a factory closes down — effect on employees, on other
employment in the town etc.
Planning local transport.
A project on attracting new work to the neighbourhood.
Planning leisure facilities
A project on broadcasting schedules.
Organizing a small business.
Local social services and their problems.
A study of newspapers and advertising.
Making a newspaper or local radio programme.

Sometimes a project would be helped by the computer as data-bank;
sometimes it would be helped by the computer providing a simulation. Some
years ago, British Petroleum, in co-operation with the Department of Education at the University of Bath sponsored a package of games relating to the
oil industry. It was a glossy and expensive pack but the simulation games were
well designed and educationally both exciting and valuable. If such a package
were produced today, it would gain immeasurably by the inclusion of appropriate programs for the school micro. (We understand that this has now been
done.) Here are two examples from that pack:

1. A public enquiry simulation — the building of a North Sea oil ter-
    minal near a quiet Scottish coastal town. Arguments depend on
    striking the balance between the needs of the oil industry and en-
    vironmental considerations while national policies also play a part.
    The arguments are clear enough and the pack provides briefing.
    Better data and, one hopes, better arguments would be possible if
    players had access to a computer data bank. The simulation
    provides a good model for local issues of this kind.

2. An oil pollution game. There is a large oil slick off-shore to a
    seaside resort. The local authority has limited resources but some
    access, in time, to national assistance. The movement of the oil
    slick depends on wind and tide. As the game progresses and plans
    are made within the constraints and within time limits set by a
    tape, so the situation changes, and further information becomes
    available. The pack provides information cards on request to
    players. The whole simulation could be enriched and improved on
    computer.

Uses of the kind just described do meet the criteria for 'convergent' thinking; they also illumine genuine problems and the ways in which people go
about solving them. At the time of writing, we have no evidence that computer
programs as yet exist to assist such social studies projects; except, perhaps,
devised locally in individual schools and by individual teachers. There is enormous scope here for writers and publishers.

If computers are used as a normal teaching aid during social studies, then there should be little problem incorporating within the syllabus the kind of 'computer awareness' material we advocate. The third-year syllabus summarized above is not a bad start for thinking about the necessary revision of the curriculum. The Bryanston Seminar devoted some time to precisely this issue and, as a consequence, came up with a number of ideas about the resources that would enable a school to develop enquiry and discussion.

A School Programme for 'Computer Awareness'

Before elaborating upon the kind of awareness programme which is needed, we would like to make three important points.

First of all, there is not a great deal of point in exploring modern and future technology without having some of it around! Nevertheless, our suggestions involve not only some material for a microcomputer but also the use of tape/slide material and print. A good deal could be 'home-made'.

Secondly, all resources for teaching need to take into account a wide range in both age and ability. It is worth noting, for instance, that useful work can be tackled with quite young pupils and this is a foundation for the help that needs to be offered to the 14–17 year-olds.

Thirdly, a book such as this must recognize in its suggestions the continuing pace of change. Before the end of this year of writing (1983) there will be fresh developments that will have their effect on schools as well as society, and so some of our suggestions may soon be outdated.

It is very difficult for children to appreciate the pace of change. Even so, a boy or girl of eleven or twelve can look back five years to the days before micros. TV programmes were different in some ways — there were certainly no computerized titles. The last five years have been the years of the film 'block-busters' using quite advanced technology — *Superman, Star Wars* and now *ET*. We are some way on now (technically) from even *2001: A Space Odyssey*.

How much more change have parents seen! A journey back just a few years in time will point this lesson. Pupils can begin to think of the impact of the chip in their life today — quartz watches, calculators, videos, washing machines controlled by a chip and so on. As we suggested in Chapter 1 the changes are already highly visible in any high street — travel agent, bank, supermarket.

If pupils talk to grandparents, they will get yet another perspective. The author of this chapter was born in the very early days of broadcasting and lived his childhood in a house lit by gas. There were few buses and people travelled by steam train. Holidays abroad were only for the rich. There was no TV; the cinema was silent and black and white. Few households were linked by telephone — certainly the author's house was not until the Second World War and then because of his father's work in Civil Defence.

Pupils, then, can consider change in both historical and geographical terms. Communications technology has increasingly brought this world and its planetary system within some kind of electronic understanding as cameras travel for us. There is no shortage of material to illustrate these points — talking to people, old magazines (the library can help), old books, old photographs, some museums and so on. Good use can be made of maps; a modern atlas (e.g. *Times Concise* or *Philip's Library Atlas*) will have communication maps or even maps of the moon and the solar system. If possible, pupils can compare such modern maps with those of, say, thirty or forty years ago. School bookrooms and libraries can often yield some interesting veteran textbooks and atlases!

It is worth spending some time looking at the crucial inventions and their timing. A class can construct a histogram of twentieth century change in communications. This could start with the beginnings of radio (about the same time as the internal combustion engine and early attempts at powered flight) and the crucial invention of the thermionic valve which made public radio possible.

Warfare in this century has provided impetus for technology. The First World War saw the first use of aircraft and of radio. The Second World War saw, in particular, the development of radar and the beginnings of the computer in the form of code-breaking machines — Turing worked at Bletchley Park. After the Second World War the crucial invention was the transistor. It should not be too difficult to find an example of, or even a photograph of, a radio set from the days of the valve to compare with the compactness of the modern printed circuit transistorized set. There is an interesting comparison too between an old gramophone and a modern 'music centre'.

Nevertheless, principles have not changed so much. The transistor does the same job as the valve — a gateway that can be open or closed to the passage of an electric current. The 'chip' takes advantage of special qualities in the element silicon that enables us to construct microscopically on the surface of the mineral very complex electrical circuits which, again, use the principle of the valve or electrical gateway.

In consequence, there is probably little need to spend much time on the 'workings' of a modern computer — at any rate, beyond the kind of block diagram found in the average micro manual. If a Sinclair Spectrum is available, there is a useful introductory program that offers a basic understanding of how a computer works. If a class understands that a computer is basically an information processor, then it should be possible to go on to illustrate the common uses of the machine. It is important, though, that pupils understand what is meant by a 'program' — the concept mentioned earlier in Chapter 3 of the 'incomplete machine' is helpful here.

In general, applications discussed and exemplified in a school programme for computer awareness should include:

1. *Home uses* of the micro-chip: the programmed washing-machine, oven, etc. Control systems that can be made available in the home — central heating, for example. How would people welcome robots in the home? The links between video and computer via cable or satellite. Interaction — shopping and banking without moving. Mention has already been made of Asimov's 'The Fun They Had'.[5] Older pupils will find much to discuss in E. M. Forster's *The Machine Stops*.[6] Is it prophetic?

2. *Teletext Systems*: Introduced in Home Uses. However, as Chapter 5 suggests, it is important that pupils learn to cope with such systems and make effective use of them. In Social Studies, discuss the possible changes such information systems will bring — on printed newspapers, on current TV systems (including news), on books, on opinion polls and voting.

3. *Information and Ourselves*: Do pupils appreciate how much information is on record about themselves? Consider birth certificates, etc. Then there are the various licences we need; who sends the reminders and how do they know when to send them? There are medical records (GPs and sometimes hospitals), insurance records (in a job, National Insurance; out of a job, benefit records), police records (for some of us — who?) and, of course, there are school records. Most of these records are kept by official bodies. What about the 'unofficial records'? Consider, for example, those kept by credit card companies, banks, shops for their credit customers, mail order companies (check for personal experience there). How can we know what is entered under our names? What rights have we? What happens if wrong information is put on a computer? What safeguards do we want? Resources here can include examples of computerized data about people and, if possible, an example on the school computer of a pupil file.

4. *Changing Patterns of Work*: In any senior class in a secondary school, there will already be some experience. There will be fathers, uncles, aunts, older siblings with experience of job changes, redundancy and so on. To what extent have family friends and relations been directly affected by technological change?

A good deal has been said already to indicate the necessary areas for discussion. It should be possible to demonstrate some examples of automation (in the forms of both control technology and word processing). It would be valuable to devise a simulation game (ideally with computer programs to supply data) on automation in a factory, an office or a shop. Office equipment manufacturers will have material (including photographs) on their products in the modern office.

Will automation permanently destroy jobs? Do we face a future in which all of us will have a good deal more disposable time? What personal skills might prove particularly helpful? (e.g. not just the skills of looking after electronic machines but some service skills and, we would argue, a number of traditional craft skills — woodwork, horticulture, cookery and a range of other crafts — as well as skills in looking after people and animals). What is likely to be the future of the city? Consider the modern city with its concentration of office blocks (how long a life do they have?) and shopping centres. What should take their place?

It is important to ensure that work in this area does not concentrate all the time on conventional work situations or so-called 'life skills' conceived as narrowly as they seem to be in 1983 MSC courses. A major purpose must be to help young people begin to identify their own strengths — what, in times of change, they might be able to do to help themselves and others. It seems to us that Social Studies, without taking a particular political stance, must be in the business of social change in (a) preventing the social consequences of technological change being in the direction of the authoritarian and (b) ensuring that society develops more democratically — that is, with people able to play a positive role and make their own decisions in life.

Work of this kind, incorporated into a Social Studies programme in schools can fit well into the curriculum as a whole. The material is plainly relevant. There is little question of prejudged answers as none of us knows how society will develop even over the next ten years. We can only produce guesses that are as informed as possible. We can do what we can to be as adaptable as possible. We can do what we can to maintain and enhance human dignity.

8

Teaching the Humanities Curriculum

Many of the teaching approaches described in the previous two chapters will also apply to the teaching of the humanities of course, especially as we have adopted a Language across the Curriculum perspective in our thinking about the teaching of English and the Language Arts in Chapter 6. But in that area of the curriculum designated 'Humanities', we often see in schools a content-heavy, information-based concept of education. Whether this should be so or not is questionable. Indeed the definition of what we mean by 'the Humanities Curriculum' is a complex one, explored in detail in Adams, *The Humanities Jungle*.[1] It is not our intention to reopen this discussion here but rather to consider more distinctive possibilities for the use of microcomputers in the teaching of History, Geography and related subjects. In what are still, in their teaching, subjects much concerned with information, the new computer and microelectronics science of 'informatics' ought certainly to have a part to play. Of course, such subjects are also necessarily much involved with language and communication. A good deal of what has been said in Chapter 6 will apply here also, notably the implications of the use of the microcomputer as a word processor. We restrict our discussion here to those possibilities that have not been extensively explored so far in this book.

Readability and Information Provision

The humanities curriculum makes a good deal of use of books of reference. Nowhere else in the classroom from the primary school onwards is there so much need for up-to-date information and the study skills necessary to access, evaluate and use it. Our examples drawn from history teaching in Chapter 1 showed quite young children grappling with the conceptual problems created by the 1851 census and this immediately suggests one positive advantage of using a data-base for such work rather than a conventional reference book or textbook. It is impossible to browse through a data-base in the same way as a more traditional book of reference: you have actively to seek out the information that you need. As we have already seen, learning how to ask the right questions, which means defining exactly what it is one needs to know, is essential if one is to succeed in getting the answers. Hence the necessity *to think through the problem* before beginning the investigation and seeking the answers. This should be contrasted with the more familiar use of reference books in a library by students, especially those of middle or lower ability. There is some awareness that the book they are considering *ought* to contain the right answers (frequently, of course, it does not because they have chosen the wrong book in the first place) and there is a tendency to open it more or less at random, find a word or phrase that bears some resemblance to the matter to be investigated, and then to copy out undigested chunks of the text without any attempt to establish their relevance or coherence. Much 'project' or 'research' work in the secondary school suffers from this kind of approach and teachers in the Humanities are frequently seeking ways of helping students to get beyond this 'copying it out' approach. Given conventional reference sources this is exceedingly difficult. Elaborate drills have been evolved by those concerned with the teaching of so-called higher-order reading skills. For example, there is the familiar formula, SQ3R, which is designed to take students through a regular sequence of activities which will help them to find the right book ('Survey'), ask the appropriate questions ('Question'), and go through a process of reading, assimilation and reproduction in their own language ('Read', 'Recite', 'Recall'). But valuable though such a formula has proved to be in at least giving some direction to what would otherwise be an aimless leafing through books, it is a purely mechanical process and it is in no way integrally linked with the nature of the reading process itself. It is a technique, not a method. With the use of a database as a source of information a very similar process has to be gone through as we have already seen. But this time it is a method, indeed the *only* method by which the information can be obtained. So, through its use, students are led to an understanding of how the knowledge is organized and encouraged to find new ways of reorganizing it. This is especially true if the students have also been encouraged to construct data-bases of their own. The work described earlier in Chapter 5 where we are exploring study skills has, therefore, a particular relevance to the humanities curriculum. A necessary further task is to find ways of helping students to transfer their understanding of how knowledge is organized in a computerized data-base to its organization and storage in conventional books as well.

One problem with the conventional book of reference in the Humanities is that it is frequently written at a level of difficulty beyond the reading ability of the student who is trying to use it. In the telling phrase used by reading specialists such a student is working at 'frustration level' and it is this which so often leads to a copying out of irrelevant chunks of text in the hope that they may make some sense. Such students can 'decode', that is read the actual words on the page; what they cannot do is to put them together into any form of meaningful discourse. There has been, in consequence, in recent years much interest in the concept of 'readability', and the various formulae whereby it should be possible to ascertain (albeit very roughly) whether a test is likely to be suited to the age and ability level for which it has been selected by the school. Studies which have been done on readability on an extensive scale show that secondary schools typically use books that are at least two years too advanced for the reading age of their pupils. To let a student loose in a library filled with reference books is, of course, to compound this problem. It is no uncommon sight to see a student with a reading age of 12 or less, leafing through a volume of the *Encylopedia Britannica* and making very little use of it. There is a very useful and full discussion of these issues in Harrison, *Readability in the Classroom*[2], where the variety of tests of readability that exist are explored and their uses and dangers analysed. By far the most accurate means yet available to us of assessing readability is to use a computer program, such as the STAR program listed in Harrison's book. With this, and other programs of a similar kind, we can find more effective means of matching student and book, especially if we test the individual student on a reading age test which can itself be computerized. Similarly, if we are writing, it is now possible to obtain a word processing program that will give us regular information about the reading level of the text that we are typing in, or that will monitor our use of language, warning us if we are using too many polysyllables or repeating the same word too frequently.

If such programs are sensitively employed (which means with a writer's and teacher's eye and instinct and not in a purely mechanistic way) we should be able to improve considerably our judgement about the text which we present to students, and also to improve greatly the written work-sheets that we so often prepare for them in the humanities lesson. At present the main problem in using the computer program to assess the readability of printed text or to help us to write our own materials to a given readability level is the time taken to input the text for analysis. However, this is likely to be overcome very soon. It is already technically possible to use the process of Optical Character Recognition, (OCR) although at present the facility for doing so is somewhat costly. The cost is expected to drop dramatically in the near future, however, and this will bring the technique within easy reach of every school with microcomputing facility. By OCR, we mean a process whereby the microcomputer can 'scan' natural text in its printed form and 'read' it into the computer's memory. In other words, it will be possible to use a program that will assess the readability of a text without the necessity of typing in the material at all. This should make the selection of reference books and the writing of home-produced materials much more effective than ever before in terms of matching the level of difficulty of the text to the ability of the students. In the next stage of development the same optical system will be able to recognize and interpret hand-written texts. It is likely that students will be able to conduct experiments on their own work and that of their peers and get stylistic feed-back on the writing techniques they have employed.

There are two further problems currently associated with the use of reference books in a library. One is the dated nature of much of the information they contain; the other, the problem of helping the student to identify the right book in the first instance.

We need, of course, to try to train students to check the publication date of reference material they are using and to realize that the information contained in, say, a gazetteer published six years ago is of dubious validity today. But this is a very difficult concept to get across and, even if we are successful, *every* reference book is bound to some extent to be out-of-date as soon as it is published. In trying to extract figures to illustrate our argument in Chapter 2 we were constantly frustrated in this way. The latest figures available to us were always considerably out-of-date and would be even more so by the time this book was published. But with computerized information this problem disappears. There is no difficulty in constantly updating the information that is being provided and with the increasing use of PRESTEL, which we expect to see widely used in the next few years as the system becomes cheaper, it should be possible for students working on Humanities projects to get absolutely up-to-date information rather than rely upon that contained in out-dated books of reference. There is an important economic consideration here also. Reference books are expensive to buy, become obsolete very quickly, and are quite useless when this happens. Hence many school libraries are still making use of what are essentially historical curiosities such as the eleventh edition of the *Britannica*. PRESTEL may *seem* expensive but the fact that the information content can be continuously upgraded makes it, even today, a worthwhile investment. Working last year with a group of students on aspects of the politics of the European Economic Community we were able to get information that was no more than twelve hours old and, indeed, to get a printout of part of a pamphlet published that morning by a European MP, something that no library of reference material could have made possible. In strongly information-dependent areas of the curriculum the value to students of being able to obtain up-to-date and accurate information of this kind goes without saying.

Computerized storage of information is not only accurate but is also economical of space, another problem with the conventional reference library. We can simply access the information that we need as we need it. In the conventional library the average student is confronted by so many books that it is difficult to know where to begin. Hence the tendency to grab anything that looks remotely relevant in a kind of blind panic or to adopt a tactic of aimless browsing. The now very dated, but still much used, Dewey Decimal system of classification and the arrangement of the conventional library catalogue do not help very much. We can now envisage computerized library catalogues where students will be able to go to a terminal, type in a list of features that interest them about a particular topic, and be instantly directed to the library's holdings in the area, together with any relevant cross-information.

We would not want to suggest by the foregoing that the conventional library is out of date, although certain kinds of reference books (telephone directories, for example) are bound to be rendered obsolete by computerization. But the proper use of computerized information data-bases should make students more aware of the ephemeral nature of much that passes for 'knowledge', more capable of handling projects within the Humanities programme, and (in the end) more efficient users of conventional libraries and reference books as well.

Games and Simulations

We have already discussed extensively the use of interactive games to develop language and thinking skills amongst students. But games and simulations are much used in Humanities subjects, such as Geography and History, to try to lead students towards conceptual understanding also. A whole literature exists on the value of this approach to education, see, for example, Taylor and Walford.[3] It seems an easy extension to adapt many of these games to the microcomputer with all the advantages provided by moving and colour graphics and the motivation they can provide. We have seen a number of examples of programs especially written in the form of geography and history games. Thus there is a listing in Payne *et al*[4] of a history simulation entitled 'DRAKE' which it is claimed is:

> a decision-making simulation in which students are encouraged to role-play with a view to gaining an insight into a historical situation and also to establish empathy with the central character . . . The computer has stored, *as well as the research of the programmer will allow*, the story of Drake's voyage round the world. Unlike a conventional text, it interrupts the reader every so often and says something like, 'What do you think of that?' or 'What would you do next?' What we have is a dynamic text. In its limited way the book 'talks' to the reader. It listens to the answer and comments upon it.
>
> (our italics)

What actually happens is that the program, accompanied by a map tracing Drake's voyages, tells the story in outline stopping at various points where decisions have to be made and requires the student, or group of students, to decide what course of action to follow next. In practice, however, in spite of the claims that are made in the above-quoted passage, the actual program is somewhat disappointing. It tends to end up much like a multiple-choice quiz in which the students try to 'guess' the 'right' answer rather than work through the actual decision-making process. Here is an extract from the beginning of the sample run quoted by Payne:

```
PLOT/LOG        SET SAIL FROM PLYMOUTH. 13TH DEC. 1577
                REACH MOGADO 27TH DEC.
                HERE YOU TRADE WITH THE MOORS. CAPTURE SPANISH
                MERCHANT SHIPS. REPLACE THE CHRISTOPHER WITH THE
                CAPTURED BENEDICT.
TYPE CON WHEN READY TO CONTINUE
-CON

PLOT/LOG        SAIL TO ISLAND OF MAYA (CAPE VERDE ISLANDS)
                CAPTURE PORTUGUESE SHIP LADEN WITH PROVISIONS.
                PLACE A CREW OF 28 ON BOARD UNDER THE COMMAND
                OF YOUR CLOSE FRIEND THOMAS DOUGHTY.
TYPE CON WHEN READY TO CONTINUE
-CON

PLOT/LOG        SAIL TO RIO DE LA PLATA. ARRIVE APRIL 5TH.
                SAIL TO PORT SAINT JULIAN. ARRIVE 19TH JUNE
TYPE CON TO CONTINUE.
-CON

DECISION 1      DOUGHTY HAS BEEN STIRRING UP TROUBLE AMONGST
                THE CREW. HE HAS TRIED TO UNDERMINE YOUR
                AUTHORITY AND RAISE MUTINY (A TREASONABLE
                OFFENCE) AMONGST THE CREW WHO ARE ALREADY
                ANGRY AT HAVING BEEN TRICKED. DOUGHTY
                HAS PROBABLY BEEN PERSUADED TO DO THIS BY
                LORD BURGHLEY WHO WOULD LIKE THE MISSION
                TO FAIL BECAUSE HE DOESN'T WANT TO STRAIN
                RELATIONS BETWEEN ENGLAND AND SPAIN.

DO YOU     (A)  SEND DOUGHTY BACK TO ENGLAND IN ONE OF THE SMALL
                SHIPS SO THAT HE CAN BE OF NO FURTHER TROUBLE.

           (B)  GIVE HIM A PUBLIC WARNING IN FRONT OF THE CREW
                TO THE EFFECT THAT ANY FURTHER TROUBLE WILL BE
                DEALT WITH SEVERELY.

           (C)  TRY DOUGHTY FOR TREASON AND EXECUTE HIM IF
                FOUND GUILTY.
TYPE A, B OR C
-C
(C)    PROBABLY A WISE DECISION.
       DRAKE THOUGHT SO.
       THE CREW WERE A ROUGH CROWD.
       DRAKE APPEARS TO HAVE THOUGHT IT NECESSARY
       TO TAKE A VERY STRONG LINE.
       HE COULDN'T AFFORD TO SHOW ANY WEAKNESS IN FRONT OF
       A DISCONTENTED CREW, EVEN IF IT INVOLVED THE DEATH
       OF HIS FRIEND. HE WOULD FIND IT DIFFICULT TO EXPLAIN
       TO THE QUEEN WHY HE HAD NOT TRIED DOUGHTY FOR
       TREASON AS IT WAS HIS DUTY.

DECISION 2      THE FLEET IS TO SAIL DOWN THE COAST
                AND THEN THROUGH THE STRAITS OF MAGELLAN
                INTO THE PACIFIC. THE STRAITS IS A DIFFICULT
                PIECE OF WATER AND ROUGH SEAS ARE EXPECTED.
DO YOU     (A)  TAKE ALL THE SHIPS THROUGH.
           (B)  BREAK UP THE SWAN, THE BENEDICT AND THE
                CAPTURED PORTUGUESE VESSEL AND DISTRIBUTE THEIR
                SUPPLIES, USEFUL EQUIPMENT AND CREW AMONGST
                THE OTHER SHIPS.
TYPE A OR B.
-B
(B)    UNDER THE CIRCUMSTANCES, A GOOD DECISION.
       IT IS QUITE LIKELY THAT ONE OR MORE SHIPS WILL BE
```

BADLY DAMAGED, SUNK OR SEPARATED FROM THE REST.
IF THE SUPPLY SHIP IS LOST THIS WOULD CREATE SERIOUS
PROBLEMS FOR THE REMAINING CREWS.
DRAKE CLEARLY BELIEVED IT UNWISE TO HAVE ALL HIS EGGS
IN ONE BASKET AND ORDERED THAT THE SWAN AND THE
SMALLER SHIPS SHOULD BE BROKEN UP.

PLOT/LOG   THE PELICAN, ELIZABETH AND MARIGOLD SET SAIL
                  FROM PORT ST. JULIAN 17TH. AUG. ARRIVE AT THE
                  STRAITS OF MAGELLAN.

DECISION 3.   BEFORE ENTERING THE STRAITS, DECIDE
                  WHICH SHIP YOU WISH TO SAIL IN.
WILL YOU SAIL IN (A) THE PELICAN.
                 (B) THE ELIZABETH.
                 (C) THE MARIGOLD.
TYPE A, B OR C

While we would not wish to be too dismissive of what is a pioneering program of its type, there seem to us to be two problems here which future simulation designers need to take into consideration. First, the students working through the simulation are not really in possession of sufficient information to make sensible decisions — it is difficult to see what else they can do other than guess in the above example — and, secondly, the simulation as a whole leads mainly to gaining knowledge of *what actually happened* rather than understanding *why it happened*. It still suffers from the basic problem of so many Humanities curricula of being primarily concerned with information acquisition. Furthermore, as indicated in the emphasis we have added to the first quotation above, the design of the program depends upon the historical research and understanding of the writer of the program. It is the teacher who has done the real historical investigation here (or taken one over ready-made from other sources); it does not lead to any genuine historical investigation on the part of the student.

The other major weakness in programs of this kind seems to be that the decision which is made has no effect on the further progress of the simulation. The student is simply told whether he has made the right or the wrong response. If we are actually to learn from simulations of this kind they need to be designed in more complex ways so that the consequences of decisions that we make affect the progress of what happens next. In this way, if disaster overtakes the voyagers because of the decisions that we have made, we may be motivated to go back and see what Drake actually did and how he evaded disaster and then be in a position to evaluate our responses alongside his. There is, of course, no necessity to suppose that Drake's real-life decisions are any more likely to be 'correct' than ours in working through the simulation. The notion of 'correctness' does not seem a particularly helpful one here. What we should be concerned with is the understanding of the processes involved. We are reminded here of Aristotle's dictum that poetry contains more truth than history since history only tells us what happened whereas poetry tells us what ought to have happened. The good Humanities simulation seems to us to need to share this quality and to leave room for the imagination and exploration of the student and not be totally dependent upon purely storing information *as well as the research of the programmer will allow.* If the program is to be genuinely educational, it ought to allow scope for both the imagination and the research of the student as well as that of the programmer.

Of course, such problems are not limited to computerized simulations. What we have been talking about is endemic in all simulation approaches to highly complex real-life situations. The problem with war games, for example, is that we are never in possession of all the relevant information that led Wellington to fight the battle of Waterloo in a particular way. There is a very real danger of over-simplifying exceedingly complex issues. In a useful discussion of the advantages and dangers of computer-based simulations Doerr comments:

> . . . students tend to think that because they understand the simple represen-
> tation of the real life event, they also understand all the real phenomena
> similar to it. Thus if they understand a simulation of political campaigns in
> the 1928 election, they think they can fully evaluate influential factors in the
> 1976 election − when in truth radically different forces were at work in the
> two elections. Another problem is compensating for the inevitable bias of the
> designer of the simulation.[5]

Of course such dangers exist in the use of all forms of classroom simulation. But the added motivational power of the microcomputer and the vividness that it can impart to a simulation make it all the more necessary for us to be wary about its misuse in the computerized humanities classroom.

There is also an important distinction to be made between games and simulations in the classroom. In a simulation we are producing something that approximates to reality; in a game we are liberated from reality and simply have to operate within the rules imposed by the game itself. A game, therefore, sets up a more closed universe than a simulation but one in which we are freer to explore the system that the game has created. In a game, too, there is usually some sort of contest, for either players compete with each other, or one or more players compete with the machine. In a game, then, it is generally poss-ible to know whether you have been successful, whether you have 'won' in fact. In a simulation this is less so.

Our own experience leads us to believe that, especially in computerized form, games are likely to be more educationally useful than simulations in the Humanities classroom, especially when the student is led to explore the val-idity of what has been learned from the game to the real-life situation afterwards. Games provide, in fact, something like a controlled laboratory situation: we can try things out in a limited environment and then, afterwards, see how the lessons learned can be applied on a wider basis. Doerr[6] provides a helpful summary of the value of games in the classroom:

1. Students like them and look forward to them.

2. Games can be played by groups of students as teams, with all the socialization to be gained from competitive interaction among peers. Cooperation is necessary for success and discipline is self-imposed by having to play by the rules. The games are student-centred and student-managed, with little interference from the teacher.

3. Games help develop decision-making capabilities and problem-solving skills, as well as encourage imaginative and creative responses.

4. Games introduce new ideas. They are open-ended and can be modified for use for a multitude of purposes.

5. Games can expend the attention span of students as a result of intense involvement in a goal-directed activity.

6. Games can be made relevant to students' lives or backgrounds, orientated to any chosen problem area, or related to a totally imaginative situation, depending on the desires and needs of the teacher and the students.

In Chapter 6 we explored some of the ways in which games can help in teaching the Language Arts using the microcomputer; there is no reason why similar games cannot be developed in the Humanities areas of historical and geographical study. Indeed, the 'game' in this sense may be likened to the widespread use of the 'model' in social science investigations. Using the computer we are able to work with and manipulate the model prior to testing it against the more complex nature of reality to see if it provides genuine illumination. The advantage of using a computer in this way is that, if it fails to provide the insight looked for, we can always reprogram and start again.

One idea recently suggested to us, for example, would involve the planning of a journey, using a real or imaginary map, with lots of information being supplied in the form of timetables, costs of various methods of travel and so on. The situation could be varied by the student being given a certain limit on the time and money available for the completion of the journey and various hazards, such as missed connections, could be built into the game on a randomized basis. Through a game such as this, the layout and geographical disposition of a real or imaginary country could be explored and the 'real-time' distances in terms of travel as opposed to the physical distances as shown on the map could be explored. One could envisage a game such as this playing an important part in introducing students to complex issues in, for instance, the geography of communications.

Another possible exercise of the same kind might revolve around weather forecasting with the student being supplied with weather maps and other necessary information and then being required to forecast what is going to happen next. The advantage of using the microcomputer in all games of this kind is both its capacity to constantly update the information and its interactive capacity so that inputting a solution to the immediate problem creates the conditions under which the next phase of the game will take place.

There are a number of commercially available educational games already on the market for History and Geography teaching which would certainly benefit and become more adaptable by being computerized. These will include many games of skill and judgement like for example the well-known North Sea Oil game. We are likely to see, with the increased availablity of micros in schools, the development of more games of this kind adapted to the use of the computer. But their educational value will depend essentially on a clear definition by the game compilers of the educational objectives that they have in mind. There is, at the moment, a considerable danger of the pursuit on the one hand of the glossy graphic for its own sake ('the machine arcade game' as applied to education) and, on the other, of the educational quiz game ('the Mastermind' approach). Neither of these two approaches seems to us to be likely to advance the cause of either Humanities education or that of the sensible use of microcomputers in schools. There is probably no other area of the curriculum nor of computer application where careful evaluation in terms of the educational benefits that will accrue from the adoption of a game or simulation is more crucial.

Specific applications

We have not attempted in this chapter to provide a detailed discussion of the use of microcomputers in the teaching of particular Humanities subjects, such as History and Geography. We are not specialists in those subject areas and it is our impression that much still remains to be done in the development of appropriate software before we can fully appreciate the potential applications. But certain things do seem reasonably clear. In geographically-based investigations, for example, the microcomputer is likely to be most useful in areas concerned with the development of skills, such as map reading and graphicacy, and in those areas which require data processing and manipulation, such as issues concerned with population growth and food resources, where the computer can do the arithmetic for us and make forecasts as to the likely outcome of possible courses of action. As is often the case, the microcomputer in the classroom can provide students with opportunities to try things out in ways not at all dissimilar to the ways in which the computer is used in real life. Such computer projections are, after all, a fact of everyday life in present-day economic planning. It remains important, of course, that the students (and the planners) regard the outcome of such predictions with a certain scepticism. Learning the fallibility of such projections is an important by-product of computer education of this kind.

The same is true in the field of History. Those who wish to learn more should look at a very useful small pamphlet published by the Historical Association, *Computers in Secondary School History Teaching*.[7] This explores the use of the computer in local history, in data-bases and simulation for the history classroom, and in the storage and retrieval of resources. Among much else, it contains a very full account of the history element in the Schools Council Computers in the Curriculum Project. Particularly interesting is a rationale presented for the use of computers in simulations.

> One advantage of the medium is that it captures attention and arouses interest and enthusiasm. This is at least in part attributable to the fact that the pupil is interested to discover what consequences flow from his own decisions. As has been said, this is particularly attractive when the nuts and bolts of the process are hidden inside the black box. In taking decisions and observing the consequences the student is in fact manipulating the model and discovering its properties — an educationally sound way of learning. The computer provides the unique facility of enabling the simulation designer to hide all or part of the rules in the black box, so that they are only discovered as the game progresses. For example, the promoters of early railways will not know until they actually build their lines what traffic they will attract from each town. In contrast, it is difficult (though not impossible) to arrange a manual simulation where players do not need to know all the rules in order to play — unless the teacher has to intervene in particular stages, which might involve a considerable burden of supervision.

The conclusion that the publication comes to seems to us one that is valid not just for History teaching but across the whole Humanities curriculum:

> We are confident that if the computer has any place in the history classroom, then it is to enable two sorts of history lessons to work more effectively. The lesson which seeks to draw historical conclusions from information selected from a data base, and the lesson where students learn from simulating a past situation, both become more practical propositions when a computer is employed to take over the tedious routine operations involved.

The Integrated Classroom

We have frequently suggested that much of the most interesting work that we have seen in schools using microcomputers has been in primary education. There is a good reason for this. The general pattern of organization of these schools, the lack of a subject-based timetable and the use of the integrated day, is one that is amenable to curriculum change and makes more possible than in traditional secondary schools the concept of 'computers across the curriculum'. As soon as a secondary school acquires a microcomputer it is likely that it will be seen as the preserve and property of a particular subject department, and, in the present climate, this is likely to be the Mathematics or the Science department. This seems to us highly undesirable on a number of grounds. First, it is a serious limitation of the use of a piece of expensive equipment. If we are to justify the use of such equipment in schools it is important that (as in a commercial context) it receives the maximum usage. Secondly, it means that the main value of such equipment is likely to be under-exploited. If we believe, as already argued, that there are important aspects of information retrieval and data-processing that the use of a microcomputer makes possible, then these uses should be available for students whatever the subject they are engaged with. The same applies to the employment of the computer as a word-processor. This should be something to be made use of whenever the need and opportunity arises, not something restricted to the Language Arts classroom alone. Too frequently curriculum development in the secondary school has foundered on the rigidly subject-compartmentalized pattern of organization that exists in such schools. The development of a programme in the Humanities itself has suffered in this way. One of the possibilities that the introduction of the microcomputer in schools has opened up is a stimulus to the breaking down of rigid subject boundaries. At the end of Chapter 6 we discussed some of the potential for using literature about computers as part of a unit on machines and society. In our view such study can only benefit by being placed alongside studies in Social Science and History. We ought to seek ways of assisting students to see things in terms of togetherness rather than apartness. It is, in fact, an issue-centred rather than a subject-centred curriculum that is most likely to arouse motivation and interest. The great contribution that can be made here by the microcomputer is that it does not belong, properly, to any 'subject' area. We have already pointed to some of the limitations of the syllabuses that exist in the area of 'Computer Studies'. But, apart from the limited *content* of such syllabuses, there is also the danger that they will limit the study of computers and microelectronics to computer specialists in schools, be they students or teachers. This is a problem that has bedevilled so many elements of the curriculum in English schools. Just as we need to develop a programme in reading in the school as a whole rather than see reading as solely the province of the English (or, even worse, the 'Reading') teacher, so, too, we need to see the microcomputer as a tool that can be used throughout the curriculum. This is not, of course, to deny the value of having a reading specialist and a computer specialist in the school who can serve primarily as an agent of curriculum development in those fields and who can also act as an adviser and consultant to colleagues in other curriculum areas. So far as patterns of organization are concerned it does not really matter if a secondary school adopts the practice of having a computer in every classroom ready and available for use as opportunity occurs (as in some of the primary schools that we have seen) or establishes a computer centre to which students can have recourse when they need, in the same way as they might go to consult a library. What matters is that the facility should be available to them to use computing equipment at that point in their learning when its use appears to be most appropriate, not just when 'computer' appears on their timetable.

In practice it is quite likely that, in the future, schools will establish 'econet' systems with relatively cheap micros acting as terminals in each classroom interfaced wtih a master computer that can act as a file server for the various out-stations, so economizing on expensive functions such as the operation of a disc drive. We have adopted the terminology just used in this paragraph quite deliberately. Much of the use of econets that we have so far seen in schools has been conceived in terms of a 'master' and 'slave' patterning of the computers, with one computer putting out programs to a series of sub-stations on which all the students are working at the same time. This is to adopt the model of the language laboratory as a model for computer-based learning. We think that this is a mistaken model and that it is essentially the *diversity* of file-serving of which even a microcomputer is possible that makes it potentially so powerful a tool for the integrated classroom.

Teachers are likely to continue to be trained primarily as subject specialists for the secondary school. This leads to a number of difficulties so far as the development of integrated patterns of work are concerned. First of all their sense of their own identity and status is fundamentally bound up with their sense of the purity of their subject specialism and, conversely, they have a sense of inadequacy in their handling of areas outside their specialism. Hence, any move towards integration, especially in the Humanities, has been highly dependent upon resource-based learning and this has led to considerable practical problems about the organization and accessibility of resources. Projects such as the Southampton-based, Nuffield-financed Resources for Learning project and the Avon Resources for Learning Development Unit seeking to pioneer ways of making resource-based learning more possible in the classroom have generally foundered over how teachers were to organize and manipulate the resources once they became available to them. Despite this the microcomputer should prove a most powerful tool. The information that teachers need in tackling areas of the curriculum unfamiliar to them (the 'data') can all be prepackaged in computer files together with ways of interrogating these data while still allowing plenty of opportunity for individual data manipulation by teacher and pupil alike. Even with the use of tape as a means of loading the micro, and certainly with the aid of discs, the handling of information on files has been made easier than it ever was in the most fashionable period of resource-based learning in the 1960s. Consequently, teachers and students should be freed to engaged in investigations together drawing for their information upon school-based, or regional, or national computerized data-banks. If we can find a way of harnessing this important resource adequately for the needs of schools, we have more possibility than ever before of producing custom-built programmes for schools both for groups of students and for individual use. We have already commented upon the disappointingly slow development of the educational potential of PRESTEL but if we are prepared to put more money into this aspect of telecommunications for educational use, the possibilities, especially with the growth of telesoftware, of creating a national resource that can be drawn upon by schools and individuals as needed in a particular learning situation should make such an investment well worth while.

In this chapter we have been able to consider only some elements in the Humanities curriculum. We have not spoken of particular subject areas, such as Religious Education, which might, possibly, have been included under that label. Inevitably, in the present state of the secondary schools, we have tended to start our thinking, even in this chapter, in subject-based terminology. But, if our ultimate aim is in the area of social and moral education as much as in the development of individual subject expertise, then it is likely to be the cross-disciplinary areas that are of most importance. The support that computer data-bases and computer programs can supply to primarily subject-trained teachers should make a transdisciplinary approach to teaching more possible in the future. In this way the best of secondary education may come to resemble the better developments and practice of primary and middle schooling and so provide a more holistic approach to knowledge for students.

9

Future Perspectives

Throughout the writing of this book we have been conscious of being constantly overtaken by events. There is not a single chapter where we have not had to change or add material at a late stage in the composition because of rapid developments in the field. In attempting, therefore, in a final chapter to suggest some of the ways in which things may develop in the future we are certainly offering hostages to fortune. Nevertheless, we feel it necessary to record what we see, in early 1983, as the possible future of microelectronics and education. There is, of course, a sceptical voice that predicts no future. We have a colleague who has seen language laboratories and teaching machines come and go and who now looks on with worldly-wise amusement at the expenditure in our department on microelectronics and microcomputers, our collection of BBC machines, word processors, printers, our PRESTEL link, and the like. He has seen it all before. But it seems clear to us that this particular revolution in educational technology is different from anything that has preceded it. It is different because, as we have shown, it is a response (and, in many ways, a rather late one) from education to a much more far-reaching revolution in society. Most of the aids to education that have been developed in the post-war years, from the overhead projector to the language laboratory, were purely educational tools and, therefore, subject to the vagaries of educational fashion. But the microelectronic age has been developing primarily outside educational circles. The analogy is between the microcomputer and the pocket calculator rather than between the microcomputer and the teaching machine or the piece of audio-visual equipment. Indeed, we have been at pains to explore in the previous pages our conviction that to see the microcomputer only as a teaching machine, a new piece of gadgetry in the classroom, is to devalue it and to misuse, as well as to misrepresent, an expensive and adaptable piece of equipment.

So we think that the sceptical view can be safely dismissed: the microprocessor and all its offshoots are here to stay. However, the most likely developments in the design of the equipment itself — the 'hardware' — will be stimulated not primarily by education but by industrial and commercial users. There already seem to be plenty of indications of the way in which things will go. We can look forward in the very near future to hardware, especially computer hardware, becoming even smaller and much cheaper and, therefore, more widely available in home, as well as in school and office. The VDU of the future is likely to be a small piece of folding plastic that we will carry around in our pocket. Already we have had announcements by firms such as Osborne and Epsom of the genuinely portable computer (the computer in a briefcase) with keyboard, VDU, loading mechanism, and printer all built in. For some time now the main limitation on the reduction of the size of the microcomputer has been the need to build it large enough to incorporate a conventional typewriter keyboard but we have already seen the development of the Microwriter, an instrument with only five 'keys', which can give all the conventional characters of a typewriter keyboard (and more beside) and with which proficiency can be achieved with two or three hours' practice. This has with it its own built-in VDU, enabling the user to see and change what he has written, in the same way as a word processor. It can be carried in the pocket, used anywhere (it has a rechargeable electric supply) and what has been written on it can be plugged into any conventional VDU or printer for more expansive display and better production quality afterwards. At the moment equipment like this is still relatively expensive, but the news is that there will be an extensive sales campaign for the Microwriter in the latter part of 1983 and the price may be expected to topple dramatically. We have now come to take this kind of equipment for granted; yet when we first saw a very early model of the Microwriter at the Bryanston Seminar it seemed an almost unbelievable product of modern electronic technology.

The point made above about ease of use is a vital one. There has already been some experiment with the use of the Microwriter in schools, especially with pupils with physical handicaps. Because of its one-hand operation and its logical arrangement of the keys, pupils who would otherwise find impossible the physical or mental effort involved in conventional writing have been shown to make remarkable gains when taught with equipment of this kind.

More generally, extensive development is already taking place which make it more possible to educate the pupil with learning difficulties alongside his peers. Programs have been developed, for example, to help, on a highly individualized basis, the pupil who has the kind of reading problems associated with dyslexia, and it seems that, in those areas where there is a combination of mental and spatial activity to be performed, appropriate programs can be produced that will greatly assist the traditionally slow learner.

It is probable, too, that what has been developed for the home and office will quickly spill over into the schools in other ways. It took some time for teachers of mathematics to accept the positive value of the use of calculators in schools. When they were comparatively expensive items of equipment their use could quite properly be restricted on the grounds that they could not be made available to everyone. As soon as everyone did possess a powerful pocket calculator, however, there was no way in which they could continue to be excluded from the school. The same is bound to happen, in the very near future in our view, with the pocket computer. The logic of the continuing fall in price and size and the continuing increase in sales is inescapable. We shall, before very long, see every child having access to a microcomputer and word processor of some kind, probably at home, if not in school. In fact, it is likely that by the end of the eighties at the latest, most of them will be carrying their own pocket size micro to school alongside whatever other equipment they need. Because the microcomputer is, as we have shown, an incomplete machine, it will, in itself, remain educationally neutral. Its ubiquity can be turned to good or mistaken educational purposes. This points to the urgency of teachers in the humanities area of the curriculum getting together now to plan the lines on which this enormous educational potential will be developed in the future.

A further likely technical development is the increasing use of disc, rather than tape, as the means both of storing and of conveying information to the computer. This may take a little longer in terms of the bringing down of costs and most of us think that tape storage will remain dominant in school use for some time yet. However, the possibilities of econet systems, linking several microcomputers together, should make file serving and the provision of information much easier and quicker than at present. We would expect, at the very least, to see every classroom equipped with a microcomputer linked to a central store, probably in the library, on which up-to-date information could be quickly accessed as and when needed by the individual pupil or the class. Already the world of information technology has led to the coining of the neologism 'informatics', and this is a word we shall hear a good deal more of in the future. Even in our own Chapter 5 we have tended to think in terms of information accessing and using within the present context of schooling and society. Our guess is that for the future we may have to think about the whole question of using and handling information in completely different ways.

But, above all, there is the question of appropriate software. At present there is still a dearth of *acceptable* educational software. This must change rapidly before the market is flooded with software that is positively anti-educational in its implications. We have already looked at some of the issues here, especially in Chapters 3 and 4, but the solution to the problem must lie in the hands of the teachers themselves. We are going to need networks of teachers who are interested in developing ideas for software in those areas of the curriculum where they have expertise. We certainly do not expect every teacher to become a program developer — that would be a waste of time and effort — but we do need more teachers to be thinking of the kind of program that they would find useful in their classes. Because the whole field is so new to most of us and so remote from the skills we have already acquired in initial and in-service training, this is going to require lateral thinking and 'brain-storming' sessions by groups of teachers rather than work by isolated individuals. LEAs should, through their Teachers' Centres, be urgently developing computer-user groups with a specifically educational focus. For the time being this is likely, at secondary level, to continue to be done largely on a subject basis and Subject Associations have a very important part to play here. The National Association for the Teaching of English and the Historical Association have both taken important initiatives here. As we write, final preparations are being made for the 1983 conference of the National Association for the Teaching of English at which a group of interested teachers and advisers will be working for about four days on software and related issues for English teaching. It is to be expected that the results of their work will receive national dissemination in due course. Alongside this is a planned distribution to all conference members, through the assistance of the MEP, of a new book edited by Chandler, entitled *Exploring English with Microcomputers*,[1] which is designed to heighten awareness of some of the possibilities amongst English teachers as a whole. There is a need for more conferences of this kind to be held under the auspices of other Subject Associations; it is probably through them rather than through the specifically computer-orientated organizations such as MUSE and MAPE that the real growth in appropriate software will come. This is, in many ways, highly desirable since we have taken the view throughout that the microcomputer should be seen as part of a 'package' of classroom learning materials rather than as something isolated in its own right. If 'user-groups' and Subject Associations can be mobilized in this way we should see more educationally desirable software develop apace. There is, after all, no shortage of programmers who can turn the ideas into usable materials — many of them are to be found in the upper forms of the schools! But, as so often, dissemination will remain a problem. We require urgent national investment in the educational uses of PRESTEL, which could form the basis for a national dissemination programme of computer software. It seems a pity that all the potential of Teletext and PRESTEL is at present being used mainly (outside the business community) for playing games.

It is likely that software development for education will lag behind the developments in hardware that we have already forecast. Teacher self-help will be essential if progress is to be made in this respect.

A further, and related, issue is that of the language in which programs are to be written. The computer press is regularly filled with lengthy and contentious articles proclaiming the pros and cons of BASIC but it seems to us, for all its technical faults as a programming language, that BASIC is here to stay. It is by now far too well established and too built into the dominant hardware to effect a change now. But there are other important considerations alongside this. Seymour Papert has frequently stressed the importance of giving very young children the experience of programming and his own language, LOGO, is quite capable of being used and producing valuable results with very young children. One of the early pieces of software development for the BBC Computer was a LOGO program and we are likely to see, alongside BASIC, more development of programming languages which can be handled by young pupils so that they can understand at least the fundamental principles which are involved. We need, in fact, to develop in pupils the *thinking skills* that are involved in programming if they are to grow up understanding, and therefore having power and autonomy in, the computerized world of the future.

One of the features of LOGO is its capacity to handle graphics and spatial concepts; see Papert's chapter on 'Turtle Geometry' in *Mindstorms*. In another chapter, 'Languages for Computers and People,' he makes the vital point:

> A very important feature of work with computers is that the teacher and the learner can be engaged in a real intellectual collaboration; together they can try to get the computer to do this or that and understand what it actually does. New situations that neither teacher nor learner has seen before come up frequently and so the teacher does not have to pretend not to know. Sharing the problem and the experience of solving it allows a child to learn from an adult not 'by doing what teacher says' but 'by doing what teacher does'. And one of the things that the teacher does is pursue a problem until it is completely understood. The LOGO environment is special because it provides numerous problems that elementary schoolchildren can understand with a kind of completeness that is rare in ordinary life.

We have seen the development of other languages that are capable of being handled by elementary schoolchildren alongside LOGO. For example, PROLOG, which is especially useful for data-base handling, has its committed supporters. It is strongly advocated for use in historical and social studies programs by historians such as Richard Ennals of Imperial College, London, for example. Like LOGO it has the advantage that it is easily learned and used by young children and it can enable them to quickly develop programming and associated thinking skills for themselves. Both languages also lend themselves to group work, unlike BASIC, which tends to be more adapted to individual work. We would certainly not expect all children to learn to program but we would expect that, in the future, many children will have learned the basic principles of programming before they arrive at secondary school.

At another level we shall see rapid developments towards programming in natural languages and this will make possible still more opportunity for pupils to take control over the direction and speed of their own learning. We are also likely to see rapid developments in voice-activated computers and the use of speech synthesizers. (Already voice-activitated typewriters are with us and talking watches and clocks are becoming commonplace.) A visionary paper by Dr Glenn Cartwright of the University of McGill, entitled *Educational Computing in the Distant Future*[3] goes even further in its description of the 'mind-activated computer'. Drawing upon evidence from current microelectronic and medical research, he argues convincingly for the ultimate development of what he calls a 'symbionic mind' which:

> may be defined as any apparatus consisting of some useful device, interfaced with the human brain, capable of intelligent action. The most difficult task in its construction will not be the creation of useful mind-expanding devices, for such simple intelligence amplifying devices like calculators and computers already exist; the most difficult task will be the design and construction of the interface unit required to link these devices to the human cortex . . . One obvious use for symbionic minds would be to enhance human memory . . . It is easy to see how people with failing memories might benefit from (an) . . . 'add-on' brain with extra memory storage . . . Never again will memories fail with age. Instead, they will improve with longevity due to better access to a larger memory store, and even the feeling of 'having something on the tip of the tongue' may disappear forever.

Cartwright goes on to discuss a range of possibilities resulting from the fact that the symbionic mind will be able to interpret our thoughts, 'our very wishes will become its commands'. Thus we shall be able to instruct it to take dictation from our thoughts, receive radio and television signals without the need for a receiving apparatus but directly in the brain, and even use our symbionic mind in the form of a 'thought switch' to control household appliances such as lighting and cookers by merely thinking about them. The whole paper is a fascinating glimpse of a possible future and one that follows logically enough from tendencies that are already with us and in current development. But, even if we regard the onset of the symbionic mind as something as unlikely as the positronic brains of Asimov's robots, Cartwright's final conclusions seem equally valid for today:

> Whole areas of curriculum will have to be re-evaluated and perhaps even replaced. We will not only change the *way* we teach, but *what* we teach as well. We will have to ask ourselves, 'What facts do we teach to pupils who are already in communication with vast data-banks? What maths tables do we teach to those who can already perform instant error-free calculation? What library skills will be needed by children who already know how to summon any document instantly to their view? What languages do we teach to those who have access to instant machine translation? What letter-writing skills will be required by students who are already in instant world-wide communication with one another?'
>   The implications for classroom teachers are . . . vast. Their role will change significantly. They will become true managers of learners rather than information amplifiers.

Certainly the possibilities of enabling people to 'plug in' at whatever age to 'learning networks' of the kind envisaged by Ilich in *Deschooling Society* is already a real possibility though, as we have seen earlier, there are good reasons for hoping that the purposes of social education will continue through some form of institution for learning even if it is very unlike a 'school' as we know it at present. Papert himself has argued[5] that computers could become powerful key resources for deschooled communities. Through a national organized data-base those who wish to acquire skills could be put easily into touch with those who wished to share their skills with others. The implications of this for the organization of a society in which knowledge is a commodity to be shared with others rather than transmitted through a downward hierarchy is a thought-provoking one which could have economic as well as intellectual possibilities. At the very least we may expect the movement towards the community school to be accelerated, more sense of education as a lifelong activity, and 'schools' becoming more like educational centres where the 'plugging in' to the national and international learning network is made possible. It is true that we have a long way to go before this is achieved. Even Papert has written: 'Faced with a computer technology that opens the possibility of radically changing social life, our society has responded by consistently casting computers in a framework that favors the maintenance of the status quo.'[6]

But, as we have tried to show in the early chapters of this book, there are strong economic and social pressures that may well mean that we shall have to radically reorganize society if we are to survive at all. It may no longer be possible, indeed, to go on with the maintenance of the status quo. It is the nature and direction that change will take that is important. This is why we believe that teachers as a whole need to be professionally informed about the matters we have dealt with in this book. The one thing that is quite clear is that the future of educational computing will be very different from the present. As Cartwright puts it at the end of his paper: 'That future is ours to plan, and ours to choose'.[7] With such sentiments we can only wholeheartedly agree.

Appendix 1:
Micro-electronics and the
Humanities

Seminar sponsored by Bryanston Audiovision at Cambridge University Department of Education from 23 – 25 October 1981

During the seminar, progress was made towards a definition of the potential and limitations of microprocessors in the Humanities. Use was then made of this definition in framing specific proposals for the marketing of software and related resource material such as books, workcards and audiovisual packages. Given the use made in computer programming of algorithms and flow charts,

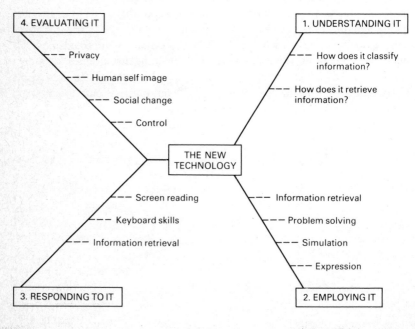

perhaps the most appropriate way of indicating how the new technology might influence humanities teaching is in diagrammatic form. For those still wedded to the old technology, the bulk of this report will be in continuous prose written, initially, with pen and paper.

In the report, the commercial potential of each of the areas indicated above is considered alongside the educational issues that are raised. The following 'principles' should, however, be borne in mind:

1. The materials should be for all children and not just the selected few.
2. We want to help teachers to use programs and not necessarily for them to become programmers themselves.
3. There is a serious danger of the home education market being flooded with bad programs based on crude behaviouristic models. Good programs for use in schools should not ignore the home market.
4. Programs for educational use will not, by and large, be self-contained but will be linked either with conventionally published material or relevant group/classroom activities. In the past, it has often been the production of self-contained educational programs that has led to the proliferation of bad CAL.

1. Understanding

In the context of Humanities, this refers to an understanding of the *use* of the technology, not the technology itself. Work was done in the seminar on ways of introducing children in primary schools to an appreciation of how the computer can store and classify data. It was suggested that classes should be encouraged to build their own and interrogate each others' data bases. These data bases, it was felt, should be carefully tailored to match the ability level and interests of the children involved. Infants, for example, might be encouraged to work on 'animals' or 'our class'. The following programme of work was outlined:

1. Introducing the Package. A starting point might well be a '20 questions' type game based on the children in the room, allowing Yes/No answers about them, which draws attention to the way in which information can be classified in sets. The computer would then be used with an introductory program illustrating the uses to which this technique can be put. The program might, for example, ask the children about themselves and then automatically interrogate the data base it has provided for itself. The program would need to be constructed so as to provide a fairly vivid illustration of what can be discovered in this way. Linked material might include the publication of wall charts showing how information about other subjects (e.g. animals) can be classified in a similar way.

2. Building a data base. In creating a data base, children would be expected to:
(a) Decide on the subject.
(b) Brainstorm to select particular features.
(c) Establish the scale of the exercise and the type of information to be fed into the computer.
(d) Collect a sample of the information and pilot its use.
(e) Test the data base.
A commercially produced program would be valuable for this work.

3. Interrogating the data base. A program for interrogating the data base should ensure that there is no ambiguity over how to consult the computer and what information the data base contains. Teachers must also be able to evaluate the particular program that is employed. In using the program:
(a) Children must be able to show how information can be retrieved.
(b) Children must be taught to isolate, evaluate and use the information.

2. Employing

The kinds of activities in which a computer might be employed can be categorized by reference to two variables. One is the type of interaction between the user and the machine and the other is the human situation that has created a demand for the use of a computer at all. Four kinds of interaction between user and machine were identified:

1. Information retrieval. It was felt that the information that is available from the computer comes in two forms — 'Raw Data' and 'The Electronic Encyclopaedia'. The use of commercially produced data bases would make it possible for pupils to frame hypotheses and check them out against the facts. This has not previously been possible in the classroom because of the problems of storing large amounts of information and the difficulties of human or mechanical methods of processing it. Examples of activities that would demand the use of a data base included the following:
(a) A historian might provide all the census returns of a particular area to a class who would then interrogate the data base in such a way as to build up a picture of the changing social history of the area.
(b) The English teacher might wish, for example, to ask pupils to review all the applications made for a particular job (e.g. looking after children in care). The pupils would be expected to filter the applications in order to

arrive at a shortlist on which they might be expected to comment in the conventional way (i.e. as a written report).

The 'Electronic encyclopaedia' would be of value in much the same way as a conventional encyclopaedia. It was suggested, however, that a programme guide to the Dewey system would be of value in using libraries. Both uses of the computer described above demand different ways of searching for data and, therefore, demand different ways of thinking.

2. Problem Solving. Access to the computer can enable the pupil to analyse material in different ways, to take data and re-arrange it in different relationships. As well as providing ways of solving problems, this can help pupils analyse *how* they are thinking.

3. Simulation. Simulation allows the pupil to hypothesize on the basis of different models of how the world works. It allows, therefore, the construction of imaginary worlds. Imperfect data can be provided and the gaps filled in a number of different ways making use of different assumptions. Examples of value to the teacher included:

(a) Economic simulation.
(b) Historical simulation, e.g. Truman embarking upon the cold war was confronted with a series of options; these could be recreated within the computer and the consequences of them explored.
(c) Battles.

4. Computers as an expressive tool. This use of computers covers both the artistic and the functional uses of the computer in assembling words (word processor), graphics and musical sounds.

3. Responding

There was initially some uncertainty about whether the seminar was examining how Humanities teachers might *use* computers or how they would be compelled to alter their practice in response to a technology that is reshaping the lives of the children they are teaching. It was quickly acknowledged that both issues needed consideration. However, neither of the discussion groups focussed specifically on the second of these areas although reference to it was frequently made. A quote from McLuhan is perhaps useful in clarifying the issues that emerged — 'Electronic Information environments alter our feelings and sensibilities especially when they are not attended to'. The implications of this are perhaps not yet fully understood. However, it was suggested that conventional notions of literacy were being challenged and some characteristics of the 'new literacy' were identified:

1. Reading a screen demands different skills to reading more orthodox forms of print. The letters, for example, are often block capitals, premium on the memory space has affected the written style so that the language is often compressed, the amount of print that is available on the screen at one time is much less than the amount available in newspapers or books, and it frequently appears on the screen for a limited amount of time only. It was suggested that reading a VDU has to be a much more *conscious* act than reading a page.

2. Keyboard skills. The use of word processors alters attitudes towards writing. The physical formation of letters, for example, is no longer a problem as it is for some children when using pen and paper, and revising and redrafting becomes a much more attractive possibility.

3. Information retrieval. It is likely that the increased use of computers will result in an 'information explosion' and that, in future, our lives will depend on the ability to handle information successfully.

It will be necessary for children to be taught these skills and it is likely that English teachers will be expected to shoulder responsibility for teaching the new literacy, just as they are responsible for its traditional counterpart. It was suggested that there was a need for the following material to support this kind of work. Firstly, a package of information retrieval skills and information processing which might be presented in traditional book form. Secondly, a package designed to introduce data bases of the PRESTEL kind to potential users. This might be at two related levels: a starter kit for primary and middle schools which might include a piece of computer software together with work cards and teachers' material, and an extension aimed at sixth forms, colleges and INSET programmes.

4. *Evaluating*

Repeated reference was made to the way in which interest in computers has developed both within schools and in the wider community. The emphasis has been predominantly technical and often, therefore, uncritical about associated social and political questions. Four areas of concern were referred to:

1. Control. It was felt that the kind of commercial control that British Telecom (which was compared with the BBC in this respect) wields over PRESTEL raised important issues about the centralization of news gathering, the effect of the new technology on other more conventional sources of news and opinion and the problems of accessibility to a medium that demands expensive capital investment. A teaching package was proposed in the form of an A.V. presentation on the social implications of communications in the 80s from TV set to satellite.

2. Technology and Social change. In particular, it was felt that consideration was needed of the way in which the new technology alters both the kind of jobs that are available and the patterns of employment that are likely in the near future. The most far reaching changes, it was felt, would be in the relationship between home and work and, therefore, in the kind of sex roles that are widely adopted since current sex roles rely upon a very traditional notion of this relationship. Conventionally published material would be of value to support work of this kind.

3. The human self image. The use of computers inevitably raises questions about the nature of artificial intelligence and, therefore, about human intelligence. Within a discussion of this kind in the classroom, it was felt that a programme illustrating the nature of computer intelligence would be invaluable. Such a programme might, for example, demonstrate how computers can *learn* from experience.

4. Privacy. The ability of computers to store large amounts of information about people raises various spectres because of the way in which they can process this information. It was suggested that an exercise illustrating this point might involve a comparison of how various tasks can be fulfilled using, on the one hand, a filing cabinet and, on the other, a microprocessor. The difference between the two could then be used to inform a discussion about, for example, the computerization of criminal records, medical files and car registration numbers.

Implications for Educationalists

It was felt that the new technology posed a considerable challenge to the current practice of most schools. The challenge comes from several directions:

1. The microprocessor makes it possible to bypass institutionalized education by establishing skill matching programs in which individuals articulate their own learning demands and are then, by use of the computer, linked up with someone who can fulfil those demands.
2. The development of educational programs might lead to a take over of education by big business. The likelihood of such a

development would be enhanced if the current government were to endorse the use of a 'voucher' system for financing education.

3.   A society that depends upon the new technology could conceivably demand very different skills from its citizens than those taught in schools at present. It might well demand a greater emphasis on collective methods of working, divergent rather than convergent thinking and a refusal to take assumptions for granted.

Scenarios for the future such as these must be used to inform the ways in which microprocessors are introduced into the current education system. It was felt that the organization of Primary schools would raise few difficulties for the introduction of computers as aids to learning, but that the Secondary emphasis on subject disciplines would present problems. A core to the curriculum that is not subject based but which draws on a number of 'Across the Curriculum Skills' — Drama, Language, Computing — would be one way of recognizing the importance of computing as a *process*.

Appendix 2: A Note on 'Hardware'

To carry out the kind of work in Humanities teaching implied in this book, a school will certainly need some reasonably generous provision in terms of machines. It is no use having one expensive machine occasionally available in a Computer Room.

It is likely that schools will tend to buy equipment initially through the Department of Industry scheme and that this purchase will determine any purchase of further machines and, of course, of 'peripherals'.

It is our view that schools will be well advised to get the BBC machine — Model B in the Secondary school with its larger capacity and, possibly, Model A in the Primary school. Primary schools should also consider seriously the purchase of the cheaper Sinclair Spectrum which, though less flexible than the BBC machine, nonetheless provides admirably for most of the purposes we can foresee with younger children.

The BBC machine is very flexible in use. If so wanted, it can be linked together (the Econet system); good printers are available; the machine can be linked to national data-bases like PRESTEL. Furthermore, it saves and loads programs efficiently.

Currently the BBC machine is produced to accept programs in the computer language called BASIC. Chips, of course, are very complex sets of electrical circuits full of 'switches'. The chip operates through myriads of switchings on and off. If you think OFF = 0 and ON = 1, then you can see that a computer can 'understand' numbers on the binary scale. Binary numbers can be used as a code to symbolize anything that can be expressed symbolically — including words. The modern micro is, however, designed so that the ordinary user does not have to operate in binary numbers or 'machine code'. We work through a coding system or 'language' that the machine is programmed to accept and convert internally into binary numbers. There are a number of these computer languages and much effort has gone into making them as much like normal language as possible. One such language is BASIC. It does have some defects but it is easy to learn simply because the ordinary user works in familiar words and symbols. One of the advantages of the BBC machine may well be that it can readily be adapted to accept other computer languages. This will depend on what the machine is being used for as languages have been developed to meet particular needs (e.g. business). At the moment, the bulk of school programs and programs for home use are written in BASIC. If you want to learn more about actual program writing, then see Appendix 6 where we include a number of books that can help you to get started.* It is certainly valuable if some teachers in a school can acquire and enjoy this skill so that at the very least someone is able to adapt material to suit specific local needs.

Word Processing

A great deal has been written in this book about the use of the computer as a word processor. To get the best value out of this application a printer is, of course, necessary. For most school applications a dot matrix printer is perfectly adequate. Some means will also be needed to SAVE and LOAD programs. Although for professional purposes discs are essential for this purpose, they are likely to continue to be expensive to install. For schools, tape storage is reasonably adequate. Even if the school does not have a printer, some useful work can be done in terms of text editing by using the VDU alone. It is still possible to SAVE the text in its various stages of composition and for the student to recall what has been written at any time and display it on the screen.

In addition to the hardware some kind of word processing package will be needed. A number of quite simple packages (more line processors than something capable of editing and formatting text) are cheaply available for most standard micros, including the BBC Model B, but for more serious application we cannot do better than to recommend (for the BBC micro) one of the especially designed packages that consist of a ROM chip that can be inserted into the computer itself. At present two exceedingly good word processing packages of this kind are easily (and relatively cheaply) available: WORDWISE (manufactured by Computer Concepts) and VIEW (produced by Acornsoft, the same manufacturers as the BBC micro itself). Both these are easy to use and provide full editing facilities. We understand also that Acornsoft is intending to produce an educational word processing package, presumably a simplification of a system similar to VIEW that will be even easier for pupils to use.

---

* Not listed in Appendix 6, though, are the various books written by Tim Hartnell for purchasers of particular computers. There are various publishers. Look out for advertisements in good computer journals. Hartnell's books strike the authors as being clear, well-written and helpful.

Appendix 3: Criteria for the Evaluation of Software

Apart from reviews in journals, users will have, at present, to make their own judgements about whether software programs and packages will suit their purposes. Unfortunately this is a field where one is all too often expected to buy sight unseen. There is a need both for an extensive reviewing system, linked with subject as well as computer expertise, and for more possibility of ordering computer programs on an approval basis. Naturally there can be problems about the infringement of copyright but by using machine code and building in protection codes manufacturers can prevent all but the most determined pirates from stealing other people's materials.

There are a number of conventional book publishers, such as Longmans and Heinemann, who have recently entered the field of computer programs. Our experience suggests that most of these programs need to be looked at very carefully in the light of the arguments developed in this book. At the time of writing, it seems to us that, of the commercial publishers, Ginn are doing the most interesting job with a wide range of material that will appeal to teachers of the Humanities. They, and we, prefer programs which are part of larger packages with appropriate support material which, of course, requires its own evaluation.

The Educational Foundation for Visual Aids is likely, in the future, to be providing a comprehensive reviewing service based upon the experience of practising teachers.

There is, of course, no substitute for seeing programs in use in schools. This is another valuable service that can be provided through local educational user groups.

Meanwhile, since most teachers and school departments will have to make their own decisions for the time being, we suggest that the following criteria might be of help in the evaluation of software:

I. Content

i   Is the content of educational value?

ii   Is the content up to date and accurate?
iii   Is there provision for adding and updating content material?

II. *Technical Considerations*

i   Is the package compatible with the computer(s) in use and any peripherals that are also needed?
ii   Is the program easy to load and does it run immediately on loading?
iii Is the program capable of being used by students independently of a teacher?
iv   Is the program reliable and 'crash proof' in normal use?

III. *Pedagogical Considerations*

i   Is the purpose of the program clearly defined? Is it clear to the students?
ii   Does the program allow students to enter it at a variety of starting points at different levels?
iii Is the presentation of the content:
     clear
     logical
     consistent?
iv   Is there appropriate use of:
     colour
     sound
     graphics?
     Are the computer and VDU being used to handle colour, sound and graphics appropriately in the classroom situation?
v   Does the program provide diagnostic help so as to suggest further appropriate activities for the student?

IV. *Student Appeal and 'User-Friendliness'*

i   Is the program motivating to the age range(s) for which it is intended?
ii   Does the program allow for student interaction and/or creativity?
iii Is the program one that gives the student adequate and early feedback about progress?
iv   Does information about student error lead to 'prompts' so that the student can continue to proceed successfully with the program?
v   Can the student easily exit from the program so as to avoid the frustration resulting from continued failure?

vi   Does the student have control over the speed of the presentation of the program material and can material presented earlier be easily recalled to the screen?

vii   Is a typed response necessary, and can the program accept some misspellings in the student response? If so, this is a good or bad thing? (The answer to this will clearly depend to some extent on the intended instructional objectives.)

viii   Is the visual display easy to read and attractively presented?

ix   Are correct responses rewarded appropriately so as to sustain motivation?

V. Documentation

i   Is the documentation for the program, and the package of which it is a part, clear and self-explanatory?

Is it written for teachers, or pupils, or both?

Is the reading level appropriate for the intended audience?

ii   Does the package include adequate and useful support material appropriate for the age and ability range for which it is intended? Are the support materials attractively presented? May they be reproduced without infringement of copyright?

iii   Does the documentation contain practical classroom suggestions for teaching the total package as well as for integrating the computer program into the rest of the teaching programme?

iv   Does the documentation contain a range of appropriate follow-up activities?

Appendix 4: Associations

Currently, there are two major teacher associations linking those who are interested in using computers in their schools:

MUSE 'exists to help teachers and their establishments to make effective use of small systems'. It claims to be the national co-ordinating body though membership seems to be largely secondary. MUSE runs courses, develops teaching packages, runs a software library and produces a journal *Computers in Schools* published by Heinemann.

MAPE is an organization specifically for primary schools. It has run two excellent national conferences (at the time of writing) and, like MUSE, is developing a network of local groups of teachers. It produces a journal *Microscope* published by Heinemann-Ginn.

To join MUSE write to MUSE Information Office, King Edward VI Five Ways School, Scotland Lane, Bartley Green, Birmingham B32 4BT.

To join MAPE write to the Secretary (Barry Holmes), St Helens CP School, Bluntisham, Cambs.

There is growing interest in the impact of microelectronics among the well-established Subject Associations and teachers of the Humanities will now find a good deal of support from such membership in this area. The National Association for the Teaching of English (NATE) ran a special Commission on computers at its 1983 Guildford Conference, organized by Daniel Chandler — see Appendix 6 for details of the book specially published to coincide. Membership address: 49 Broomgrove Road, Sheffield S10 2NA.

The Historical Association has taken an interest for even longer, publishing a pamphlet on possibilities some years ago. There are often useful articles in *Teaching History*. For membership write to 59a Kennington Park Road, London SE11 4JH.

Both MUSE and MAPE have links with the DES-sponsored Microelectronics in Education Programme (MEP). MEP have developed a network of regional offices which can be helpful in encouraging and supporting local initiatives if they fall within the MEP remit and priorities. Information about such regional offices should be available in all schools.

Educational Foundation for Visual Aids (EFVA), 254 Belsize Road, London NW6 4BY is becoming involved in both the distribution and the publishing of microcomputer software. The Foundation has produced for use by LEAs and schools an introductory videotape on microcomputers in the classroom which is a useful starting point for in-service discussion.

BBC Enterprises distribute a number of 16mm versions of material originally prepared for television, dealing with a variety of aspects of microelectronics and education. Their current catalogue is well worth consulting to see what is available.

Appendix 5: Journals

As a visit to any newsagent will reveal, there are now a large number of magazines devoted to computers. A number are aimed at the business market and others at the home user or hobbyist. It is a good idea to look now and then at the magazine racks and buy copies as and when they offer articles of interest.

Apart from the journals of MUSE and MAPE, the authors found the following of more than just occasional value (i.e. worth thinking of a subscription).

Educational Computing: This is the only commercial journal devoted to education and is virtually essential reading. Valuable for news and advertisements as well as occasional articles. The journal suffers to some degree from a Computer Studies bias but is a useful forum and will take articles and news items from readers. Published ten times a year. 8 Herbal Hill, London EC1R 5JB.

Your Computer: In the opinion of the authors, the best of the hobbyists' journals. There are more articles of general interest than is always the case and there is some interest in education. *Your Computer* is also less given to jargon than some. Published monthly. Quadrant House, The Quadrant, Sutton, Surrey SM2 5AS.

There are also two journals specifically linked to particular machines that can be interesting and helpful: *Acorn User* (for the BBC computer) and *Sinclair User* (for the ZX81 and the Spectrum). ECC Publications, 30–31 Islington Green, London N1 8BJ.

It is also important for teachers to make use of the publications of the *Council for Educational Technology*, 3 Devonshire Street, London W1N 2BA. They publish a catalogue but there are details of recent publications in the *Education Year Book*.

Appendix 6: Bibliographical Notes

The following notes cover not only some books referred to in the text but also a number of others that the authors have found to be of some value. This is not a comprehensive list, by any means. It also excludes reference to AV materials though we strongly recommend the use of the catalogues of video-cassettes available from BBC Enterprises and Thames Television. There is a very full list of AV material in John Maddison's *Information Technology and Education* (see below).

Anthony Adams: *New Directions in English Teaching*. Falmer Press, 1982.
> The first book to begin to explore the implications of the microprocessor for the teaching of English. Contains an important early essay by Chandler on the implications of the microcomputer for the English classroom.

Iann Barrow & Ray Curnow: *The Future with Microelectronics*. Open University Press, 1979.
> Prepared for the Department of Industry by the University of Sussex. Fairly technical but a reasonable forecast of the way information technology is going.

Robin Bradbeer: *The Personal Computer Book*. Input Two-Nine, 1980.
> A useful reference book about micros and some information about what is available. Get latest edition.

Robin Bradbeer, Peter De Bono & Peter Laurie: *The Computer Book*. BBC Publications, 1982.
> A very useful introduction to computers and computing written to accompany the BBC television series, *The Computer Programme*. Admirably clear in style it explains much of the language used in more technical volumes and presents a balanced survey of what computers are and what they can do. Outstandingly well illustrated.

Alan Burkitt & Elaine Williams: *The Silicon Civilisation*. WH Allen, 1980.
> Popular discussion of the chip and its future. Useful for school library.

Daniel Chandler: *Exploring English with Microcomputers*. CET, 1983.
> A compilation produced for the Easter Conference 1983 of the National Association for the Teaching of English. The first book exclusively

dedicated to looking at the role of the microcomputer in the teaching of English from every aspect.

Daniel Chandler: *Microprimer — a Foundation for Teachers*. Tecmedia for MEP, 1983.

Part of the package of resource materials prepared by the Microelectronics Education Programme to complement the Department of Industry's Micros in Primary Schools Scheme. Quite the best practical introduction to the classroom use of the micro produced so far. Though designed for the primary school teacher, it has much to offer all teachers.

Rodney Dale & Ian Williamson: *The Myth of the Micro*. Star Books, 1980.

Another popular account of developments but concerned to put in perspective some of the wilder shores of futurology. Useful for clarifying what a machine can and cannot do.

Christine Doerr: *Microcomputers and the Three Rs*. Hayden, 1979.

An early attempt to look beyond the computer as calculator in education. Some useful ideas but largely interesting as an example of almost tunnel vision — CAL and Learning Theory.

David Ellingham: *Managing the Micro in the Classroom*. CET, 1982.

This is one of the series of MEP case studies. Though directed to the primary school teacher, there is much of value for secondary schools in terms of group work.

Alan B Ellis: *The Use and Misuse of Microcomputers in Education*. McGraw-Hill, 1974.

The date suggests a voice from the past. In fact, this thoughtful book continues to be highly relevant and ought to be read by everyone with a serious interest in the potential of the micro for education. Very much lives up to the title!

Christopher Evans: *The Mighty Micro*. Gollancz, 1979.

The book of the BBC TV series which opened the eyes of many to what was going on. Perhaps over-enthusiastic about the benefits of the chip yet probably still the best (as well as the first) of the popular accounts.

Fred Learns about Computers. Macdonald & Evans, 1981.

Jokey but well presented and simple manual on computing. A good starter for anyone interested in beginning to learn about how to write a program and to gain a clearer understanding of the machines.

Tom Forester (ed): *The Microelectronics Revolution*. Basil Blackwell, 1980.

An important source book. A collection of papers on the history, use, future and social implications of microelectronics. Prepared with support from the Department of Industry. Remains essential reading for concerned teachers.

Roy Garland: *Microcomputers and Children in the Primary School*, Falmer Press, 1982.

A collection by various writers looking at all aspects of managing and using the microcomputer in the primary classroom. It has a strong sense of practicality about it and many of its ideas are adaptable to a secondary school context as well.

Godfrey, Parkhill, Madden & Ouimet: *Gutenberg Two*. Press Pircepic Ltd (Toronto), 3rd Edition, 1982.

A fascinating Canadian look at the information 'revolution'. Much useful information, some brilliant ideas and some far-fetched ones. All in all, an important non-educationist's view from inside the industry.

Philip Hills (ed): *The Future of the Printed Word*. Open University Press, 1980.

A collection of readings from varied standpoints looking at the future of print in a time of technological change. Valuable for understanding the direction of information technology as, by and large, the book is realistic and not wholly dedicated to the machines.

JAM Howe and PM Ross: *Microcomputers in Secondary Education*. Kogan Page, 1981.

A collection of articles from the Department of Artificial Intelligence of the University of Edinburgh. Many are technical but the book is specially valuable for the contribution of Mike Sharples on 'Computers and Creative Writing'.

Dennis Jarrett: *The Good Computing Book for Beginners*. ECC Publications, 1980.

Another useful introduction which has, as its outstanding feature, a practical glossary of computing terms. The glossary is written with wit as well as insight and contains much historical material.

Clive Jenkins & Barry Sherman: *The Collapse of Work*. Eyre Methuen, 1979.

A necessary counter to some of the more optimistic pieces of futurology, let alone some of the current attitudes in government and industry. We need to plan very carefully if human costs are not to outweigh any gains; that is the message of this study from the leaders of a Union that will be much affected (ASTMS).

Ron Jones: *Microcomputers: Their Uses in Primary Schools*. CET, 1980.

Ron Jones is a pioneer of the human classroom use of the micro. This valuable publication is the result of a short period of time off from being a headteacher to investigate what was happening in schools and to think about priorities.

Ron Jones: *Microcomputers in Primary Schools: A Before You Buy Guide*, CET, 1980.

Invaluable advice from a man who knows more than most about the computer in the classroom.

Peter Large: *The Micro Revolution*. Fontana, 1980.

Another quite useful popular account with a particular interest in social implications.

Peter Laurie: *The Micro Revolution*. Futura, 1980.
> Another useful paperback, this time for the clarity of its exposition of what a computer is and does. A good first read for anyone wanting basic understanding. But order by author not title to make sure of the right book!

Alan Maddison: *Microcomputers in the Classroom*. Hodder & Stoughton, 1982.
> Examines the uses of the microcomputer in schools with examples drawn from across the whole curriculum. It also includes a useful section on the microcomputer in administration in schools.

John Maddison: *Education in the Microelectronics Era*. Open University Press, 1983.
> Considers in great detail the educational implications of the age of micro-technology and the Information Revolution and places current developments firmly within a long tradition of innovation in educational technology. Written in a humane style with a wealth of reference which makes it illuminating and refreshing to read for even the least technically minded reader. It is likely to become established as both a pioneer and a standard work.

John Maddison: *Information Technology and Education*. Open University Press, 1982.
> Sub-titled 'An annotated guide to printed, audiovisual and multi-media resources' this book is just that. The annotations are scholarly and discriminating. As a reference book, it is unique and indispensable for anyone seriously concerned.

Peter Marsh: *The Silicon Chip Book*. Abacus, 1981.
> Another paperback but useful on social and employment implications.

Andrew Nash & Derek Ball: *An Introduction to Microcomputers in Teaching*, Hutchinson, 1982.
> An excellent straightforward introduction to its subject which includes a number of sample programs and gives some good advice on program evaluation. Although it assumes no prior knowledge on the part of the reader it is a little more technical and difficult than some of the other books recommended.

Seymour Papert: *Mindstorms: Children, Computers and Powerful Ideas*. Harvester Press, 1980.
> The title says it for the ideas are powerful. A seminal book on education with whose basic approach the authors of this book are much in sympathy. Though Papert's main concern is with maths education, what is of immense value is his concern for children and creative learning. Should be in all staff libraries.

Payne, Hutchings & Ayre: *Computer Software for Schools*. Pitman, 1980.
> In effect, a report of one school's pioneering work with the micro. Certainly an advance on Doerr but the ideas should be taken as valuable starting points rather than just copied.

Joseph Pelton: *Global Talk*. Harvester Press, 1981.

Stimulating essays on futurology. It might be unwise to dismiss this set of pictures of our future but we do need to be critical about some of the attitudes on offer. Technical knowledge, etc. brilliant but perhaps socially naive.

Nicholas Rushby: *An Introduction to Educational Computing*. Croom Helm, 1979.

A valuable introduction helpful in its clarity from the Director of CEDAR (Computers in Education as a Resource) Project at Imperial College. Readers can be helped to make up their own minds as to the direction in which to go with software.

Shepherd, Cooper & Walker: *Computer Assisted Learning in Geography*, CET, 1981.

A useful CET publication discussing a number of applications — though concentrating largely on CAL and the handling of geographical data.

Alvin Toffler: *The Third Wave*. Pan, 1981.

From the author of *Future Shock* also published by Pan in the UK. Another very useful book for anyone concerned with the social implications — especially in terms of how we may work and if we may work!

Notes and References

Chapter 1

1. R. Jones (1980), *Microcomputers: Their Uses in Primary Schools* (CET), p. 7.
2. S. Papert (1980), *Mindstorms: Children, Computers and Powerful Ideas* (Harvester Press), p. 30.
3. D. Chandler (1982), The potential of the microcomputer in the English classroom, in Anthony Adams (ed.), *New Directions in English Teaching* (Falmer Press), pp. 84–85.
4. S. Papert & C. Solomon (1971), *Twenty Things to do with a Computer* (MIT, Artificial Intelligence Laboratory, Cambridge, Mass. mimeo).
5. E. G. Fubini, (1971), Education in modern society, in M. Greenberger (ed.), *Computers, Communications and the Public Interest* (Johns Hopkins, Baltimore), p. 131.

Chapter 2

1. *Time*, 20 September 1982.
2. M. McLuhan and Q. Fiore (1968), *War and Peace in the Global Village* (Bantam), p. 36.
3. R. Fothergill (1981), *Microelectronics Education Programme: the Strategy* (Department of Education and Science), p. 1.
4. R. Fothergill (1981), *ibid*, p. 2.
5. D. Chandler (1982), *Micro Primer: Study Text* (Tecmedia), p. 44.
6. M. Mead (1970), *Culture and Commitment* (Doubleday), p. 72.
7. A. G. Watts (1979), *The Implications of School Leaver Unemployment for Careers Education in Schools* (CRAC).
8. K. Valaskakis (1982), *Journal of the Alberta Teachers Association*, p. 5.
9. K. Valaskakis (1982), *ibid*, p. 5.

Chapter 3

1. MUSE (1982), *School Microcomputers: Uses and Management*.
2. A. Turing (1937), *On Computable Numbers* (Proceedings of the London Mathematics Society 42), pp. 230–265.
3. P. Venning (1978), Microcomputers in the classroom, in *Times Educational Supplement*, 20 October 1978.
4. C. Evans (1979), *The Mighty Micro* (Gollanz).
5. N. Rushby (1979), *An Introduction to Educational Computing* (Croom Helm).

6. C. Doerr (1979), *Microcomputers and the Three R's* (Hayden, New Jersey), pp. 131–32.
7. N. Rushby (1979), *op.cit.*
8. J. R. Hartley (1981), Learner initiatives in computer assisted learning, in J. A. M. Howe & P. M. Ross, *Microcomputers in Secondary Education* (Kogan Page), pp. 102–117.
9. H. Bondi, Sir (1982), Why Science must go under the microscope, in *Times Educational Supplement*, 10 September 1982, p. 4.

Chapter 4

1. D. Godfrey & D. Parkhill (eds.) (1982), *Gutenberg Two* (Press Porcepic, Toronto & Victoria, Canada), pp. 158–9.
2. M. Porat (1976), *The Information Economy Vol. 1* (Stanford University).
3. T. Jones (1980), *Microelectronics and Society* (Open University Press), pp. 162–63.
4. CRAC (1982), *English, Communication Skills and the Needs of People in Industry* (Hobsons Press, Cambridge), introductory announcement.
5. *Ibid,* p. 61.
6. L. Levi (1981), *Preventing Work Stress* (Addison Wesley).
7. R. Jones (1980), *Microcomputers: Their Uses in Primary Schools* (CET), pp. 71–72.
8. R. Jones (1982), *Microcomputers in Primary Schools: A Before-You-Buy Guide* (CET).
9. D. Chandler (1982), *Micro Primer: Study Text* (Tecmedia).
10. B. Bernstein (1971), On the classification and framing of educational knowledge, in M. F. D. Young (ed.), *Knowledge and Control* (Collier-Macmillan), pp. 47–69.
11. L. C. Taylor (1971), *Resources for Learning* (Penguin).
12. A. G. Watts (1979), *The Implications of School-Leaver Unemployment for Careers Education in Schools* (CRAC).
13. A. G. Watts (1982) in CRAC, *English, Communication Skills and the Needs of People in Industry,* (Hobsons Press, Cambridge), p. 75.
14. M. Sharples (1981) in J. A. M. Howe & P. M. Ross (eds.), *Microcomputers in Secondary Education* (Kogan Page), p. 140.
15. R. Jones (1980), *Microcomputers: Their Uses in Primary Schools* (CET), pp. 29–30.
16. R. Jones (1980), *ibid,* pp. 32–33.

Chapter 5

1. Bullock Report (1975), *A Language for Life* (HMSO), pp. 95–96.
2. Schools Council (1981), Information skills in the secondary curriculum, in M. Marland (ed.), *Schools Council Curriculum Bulletin No 9* (Methuen Educational), p. 9.
3. A. Adams (ed.), *New Directions in English Teaching* (Falmer Press), p. 5.
4. HMI (1979), *Aspects of Secondary Education in England* (HMSO) — see especially Chapter 6, *Language,* pp. 71–110.
5. Report of the Bryanston Seminar (1981), *Microelectronics and the Humanities* (See Appendix 1).

6. A. Payne, B. Hutchings & P. Ayre (1980), *Computer Software for Schools* (Pitman), pp. 229–236.
7. A. Adams, N. Butterworth & E. Jones (1979–80), *English Skills I, II, III* (Harrap).
8. E. Lunzer and K. Gardner (1979), *The Effective Use of Reading* (Heinemann, not yet published).
9. E. Lunzer and K. Gardner, *Learning from the Written Word*, publication pending (Oliver and Boyd).
10. A. B. Ellis (1974), *The Use and Misuse of Computers in Education* (McGraw-Hill), pp. 131–169.

Chapter 6

1. A. Adams (1982), *New Directions in English Teaching* (Falmer Press), p. 41.
2. HMI (1979), *Aspects of Secondary Education in England* (HMSO), see especially Chapter 6, *Language*, pp. 71–110.
3. A. Adams and J. Pearce (1974), *Every English Teacher* (Oxford University Press), pp. 47–54.
4. D. Barnes (1976), *From Communication to Curriculum* (Penguin).
5. K. Weber (1982), *The Teacher is the Key* (Open University Press), pp. 95 *ff.*
6. D. Chandler (1982), in A. Adams (ed.), *New Directions in English Teaching* (Falmer Press), p. 83.
7. P. Davies (1982), in *Times Educational Supplement*, 24 December 1982.
8. A. Adams, N. Butterworth & E. Jones (1980), *English Skills III* (Harrap), pp. 63–64.
9. D. Chandler (1982), private communication to the authors.
10. Advertisement by Melbourne House Publishers in *Your Computer*, January 1983, p. 17.
11. *Story-Trails* (Cambridge University Press).
12. M. Sharples (1981), in J. A. M. Howe & P. M. Ross (eds.), *Microcomputers in Secondary Education* (Kogan Page), pp. 152–57.
13. R. Jones (1980), *Microcomputers: Their Uses in Primary Schools* (CET), p. 81.
14. F. Smith (1982), *Writing and the Writer* (Heinemann), p. 136.
15. S. Papert (1980), *Mindstorms: Children, Computers and Powerful Ideas* (Harvester Press), p. 30.
16. D. Watt (1982), Word processors and writing, in *Popular Computing* (June 1982), pp. 124–126.
17. Cited Sharples, *op.cit.*, p. 152.
18. Sharples, *op.cit.*, p. 152.
19. J. Keen (1978), *Teaching English: a Linguistic Approach* (Methuen).
20. P. Doughty, J. Pearce & G. Thornton (1971), *Language in Use* (Edward Arnold).
21. R. Jones (1980), *op.cit.*, p. 26.
22. E. Lunzer and K. Gardner (1979), *The Effective Use of Reading*, Chapter 8 (Heinemann).
23. D. Chandler (ed.), (1983), *Exploring English with Microcomputers* (CET).
24. M. Sharples (1981), *op.cit.*, p. 142.
25. See especially J. Britton (1972), *Language and Learning* (Penguin), and J. Britton (1975), *The Development of Writing Abilities* (Macmillan).

26. J. Swift (1726), *Gullivers's Travels* — various editions. Nonsuch Press (1934), pp. 179–81.
27. I. Asimov (1950), *I Robot* (Doubleday).
28. I. Asimov (1964), *The Rest of the Robots* (Doubleday).
29. J. Patrouch (1974), *The Science Fiction of Isaac Asimov,* (Doubleday), pp. 61–62.
30. I. Asimov (1969), *Opus 100* (Houghton Mifflin).
31. *Op.cit.*
32. I. Asimov (1973), *The Best of Isaac Asimov* (Sphere Books).
33. Dale Suttleworth (1981), *Times Educational Supplement,* 2 October 1981.
34. E. M. Forster (1928), The machine stops, in *The Eternal Moment* (Edward Arnold).
35. Laurence Lerner (1974), *ARTHUR: The Life and Opinions of a Digital Computer* (The Harvester Press).
36. Laurence Lerner (1980), *ARTHUR and MARTHA: Or, the Loves of the Computers* (Secker and Warburg.)

Chapter 7

1. George Orwell (1949), *1984* (Secker and Warburg).
2. Alex Hamilton (1982), *Observer,* 19 December, 1982.
3. Medway & Goodson (1975), *Times Educational Supplement,* 20 June 1975.
4. D. Gleeson and G. Whitty (1976), *Developments: Social Studies Teaching* (Open Books).
5. I. Asimov (1973), The fun they had, in *The Best of Isaac Asimov* (Sphere Books).
6. E. M. Forster (1928), The machine stops, in *The Eternal Moment* (Edward Arnold).

Chapter 8

1. A. Adams (1976), *The Humanities Jungle* (Ward Lock Educational).
2. C. Harrison, *Readability in the Classroom* (Cambridge University Press).
3. J. Taylor & R. Walford (1972), *Simulation in the Classroom* (Penguin).
4. A. Payne *et al.* (1980), *Computer Software for Schools* (Pitman), pp. 13; 15–16.
5. C. Doerr (1979), *Microcomputers and the Three R's* (Hayden, New Jersey), p. 76.
6. *Ibid.,* p. 95.
7. Historical Association (1979), *Computers in Secondary School History Teaching,* No. 40, (CET.) pp. 23, 35.

Chapter 9

1. D. Chandler (1983), *Exploring English with Microcomputers* (CET).
2. S. Papert (1980), *Mindstorms: Children, Computers and Powerful Ideas* (Harvester Press), p. 115.
3. G. Cartwright (1982), *Educational Computing in the Distant Future* (mimeo) pp. 12, 13.
4. G. Cartwright, *op.cit.,* pp. 17, 18.
5. I. Illich (1971), *Deschooling Society* (Calder and Buyars).
6. S. Papert (1980), Computers and learning, in Dertouzos & Moses (eds.), *The Computer Age: A Twenty-Year View* (MIT), p. 73.
7. G. Cartwright, *op.cit.* p. 19.

Index